Political Innovations

Political Innovations: Creative Transformations in Polity, Politics and Policy provides a theoretical framework for studies of political innovation as well as a number of empirical studies of innovations in the way policy strategies take form, in the exercise of political leadership, in community self-organizing, in political parties, and what implications informal governance has on political innovation.

Public innovation has risen to the top of the agenda among governments all over the Western world. The message is clear: the public sector needs to become more innovative in order to meet the demands of modern society. There is also a growing interest in public innovation amongst students of public policy and governance, who are currently working to define and conceptualize public innovation, analyze drivers of, and barriers to, innovation in the public sector, and prescribe ways to make the public sector more innovative. However, researchers have so far mainly theorized, studied and analyzed issues related to innovations in public services and public delivery. Few have payed attention to the fact that public service innovation takes place in a political context, and that innovations in polity, politics and policy are fundamental aspects of public innovation. A comprehensive research agenda on public innovation should therefore include studies of political innovation.

This book will be of great value to scholars and researchers interested in Public Administration, Policy Making and Innovation, Public Governance and Political Leadership.

It was originally published as a special issue of the *Public Management Review*.

Eva Sørensen is Professor in Public Administration and Democracy at the Department of Social Science and Business at Roskilde University, Denmark, and Professor II at the Department of Social Sciences at NORD University, Norway. She has published widely within areas such as interactive governance, political leadership, and collaborative innovation in the public sector.

Political Innovations
Creative Transformations in Polity,
Politics and Policy

Edited by
Eva Sørensen

LONDON AND NEW YORK

First published 2021
by Routledge
2 Park Square, Milton Park, Abingdon, Oxon, OX14 4RN

and by Routledge
52 Vanderbilt Avenue, New York, NY 10017

Routledge is an imprint of the Taylor & Francis Group, an informa business

Chapters 1, 3, 5, 6 © 2021 Taylor & Francis

Chapter 2 © 2016 Albert Meijer, Reinout van der Veer, Albert Faber & Julia Penning de Vries. Originally published as Open Access.

Chapter 4 © 2016 Jurian Edelenbos, Ingmar van Meerkerk & Joop Koppenjan. Originally published as Open Access.

With the exception of Chapters 2 and 4, no part of this book may be reprinted or reproduced or utilised in any form or by any electronic, mechanical, or other means, now known or hereafter invented, including photocopying and recording, or in any information storage or retrieval system, without permission in writing from the publishers. For details on the rights for Chapters 2 and 4, please see the chapters' Open Access footnotes.

Trademark notice: Product or corporate names may be trademarks or registered trademarks, and are used only for identification and explanation without intent to infringe.

British Library Cataloguing-in-Publication Data
A catalogue record for this book is available from the British Library

ISBN13: 978-0-367-64612-7

Typeset in Minion Pro
by codeMantra

Publisher's Note
The publisher accepts responsibility for any inconsistencies that may have arisen during the conversion of this book from journal articles to book chapters, namely the inclusion of journal terminology.

Disclaimer
Every effort has been made to contact copyright holders for their permission to reprint material in this book. The publishers would be grateful to hear from any copyright holder who is not here acknowledged and will undertake to rectify any errors or omissions in future editions of this book.

 Printed in the United Kingdom by Henry Ling Limited

Contents

Citation Information vi
Notes on Contributors viii

1 Political innovations: innovations in political institutions, processes and outputs 1
Eva Sørensen

2 Political innovation as ideal and strategy: the case of aleatoric democracy in the City of Utrecht 20
Albert Meijer, Reinout van der Veer, Albert Faber, and Julia Penning de Vries

3 Strengthening political leadership and policy innovation through the expansion of collaborative forms of governance 37
Jacob Torfing and Christopher Ansell

4 The challenge of innovating politics in community self-organization: the case of Broekpolder 55
Jurian Edelenbos, Ingmar van Meerkerk, and Joop Koppenjan

5 Political parties and innovation 74
Carina S. Bischoff and Flemming Juul Christiansen

6 Assessing the impact of informal governance on political innovation 90
Sarah Ayres

Index 109

Citation Information

The chapters in this book were originally published in the *Public Management Review*, volume 19, issue 1 (January 2017). When citing this material, please use the original page numbering for each article, as follows:

Chapter 1
Political innovations: innovations in political institutions, processes and outputs
Eva Sørensen
Public Management Review, volume 19, issue 1 (January 2017) pp. 1–19

Chapter 2
Political innovation as ideal and strategy: the case of aleatoric democracy in the City of Utrecht
Albert Meijer, Reinout van der Veer, Albert Faber, and Julia Penning de Vries
Public Management Review, volume 19, issue 1 (January 2017) pp. 20–36

Chapter 3
Strengthening political leadership and policy innovation through the expansion of collaborative forms of governance
Jacob Torfing and Christopher Ansell
Public Management Review, volume 19, issue 1 (January 2017) pp. 37–54

Chapter 4
The challenge of innovating politics in community self-organization: the case of Broekpolder
Jurian Edelenbos, Ingmar van Meerkerk, and Joop Koppenjan
Public Management Review, volume 19, issue 1 (January 2017) pp. 55–73

Chapter 5
Political parties and innovation
Carina S. Bischoff and Flemming Juul Christiansen
Public Management Review, volume 19, issue 1 (January 2017) pp. 74–89

Chapter 6
Assessing the impact of informal governance on political innovation
Sarah Ayres
Public Management Review, volume 19, issue 1 (January 2017) pp. 90–107

For any permission-related enquiries please visit:
http://www.tandfonline.com/page/help/permissions

Contributors

Christopher Ansell Berkeley Political Science, UC Berkeley, USA.

Sarah Ayres Professor in Public Policy and Governance, School for Policy Studies, University of Bristol, UK.

Carina S. Bischoff Department of Social Sciences and Business, Roskilde University, Denmark.

Flemming Juul Christiansen Department of Social Sciences and Business, Roskilde University, Denmark.

Julia Penning de Vries Utrecht School of Governance, Utrecht University, The Netherlands.

Jurian Edelenbos Department of Public Administration and Sociology, Erasmus University Rotterdam, The Netherlands.

Albert Faber Scientific Council for Government Policy, The Hague, The Netherlands.

Joop Koppenjan Department of Public Administration and Sociology, Erasmus University Rotterdam, The Netherlands.

Albert Meijer Utrecht School of Governance, Utrecht University, The Netherlands.

Eva Sørensen Department of Social Sciences and Business, Roskilde University, Denmark. NORD University, Bodø, Norway.

Jacob Torfing Roskilde School of Governance, Roskilde University, Denmark.

Reinout van der Veer Utrecht School of Governance, Utrecht University, The Netherlands.

Ingmar van Meerkerk Department of Public Administration and Sociology, Erasmus University Rotterdam, The Netherlands.

Political innovations: innovations in political institutions, processes and outputs

Eva Sørensen

ABSTRACT
Public innovation has become a key objective for governments all over the Western world and is a growing research area among students of public policy and governance. At the heart of this new agenda is the search for ways to make the public sector more innovative. Governments and researchers alike are mainly interested in assessing and promoting innovations in public service delivery, but have paid little or no attention to the need for innovations in polity, politics and policy. This article develops a research agenda for studying innovations in political institutions, in the political process and in policy outputs. It proposes a number of research themes related to political innovations that call for scholarly attention, and identifies push and pull factors influencing the likelihood that these themes will be addressed in future research.

Introduction

Public innovation has risen to the top of the agenda among governments all over the Western world (OECD 2012; US 2012, 2013; EU-Commission 2013; UK 2014). The message is clear: the public sector needs to become more innovative in order to meet the demands of modern society. There is also a growing interest in public innovation amongst students of public policy and governance, who are currently working to define and conceptualize public innovation, analyse drivers of, and barriers to, innovation in the public sector, and prescribe ways to make the public sector more innovative. However, researchers have so far mainly theorized, studied and analysed issues related to innovations in public services and public delivery, asking questions, such as: What new services, production methods, procedures and organizational set-ups for service provision have emerged? How are the innovations produced and who is involved? Which management capacities and tool kits are used, and to what effect? What impact do different innovations have on the quality and price of public service provision (Osborne and Brown 2005, 2013; Mulgan 2014)? This burgeoning body of research on public service innovation is both valuable and relevant, as it provides important knowledge about how the public sector shapes public service innovation, as well as about how, and to what extent, such innovations affect the efficiency and effectiveness of public governance. What has so far been overlooked, however, is the fact that public service innovation takes place in a political context, and that innovations in polity, politics and policy are fundamental aspects of public innovation. A comprehensive research agenda on public innovation should, therefore, include studies of *political innovation* that I will, at this point, tentatively define as intentional efforts to transform political institutions designed to make authoritative political decisions (polity), the political processes that lead to such decisions (politics) and the content of the resulting policies (policy).

The aim of this article is to put political innovation on the public innovation research agenda by proposing a number of research themes that, in this particular day and age, call for scholarly attention and debate. Before moving on, I should clarify that public innovation, be it a service innovation or a political innovation, is not a goal in itself. It is a means to an end, which is to transform the content of what is considered as public value as well as the conditions under which this content is formulated and authorized. At a given point in time, stability may be perceived as more important than innovation in achieving this goal, and much of the time the trick is to balance the need for stability against the need for change and innovation. The new public innovation agenda is important because it demonstrates that public innovation is actually an option. This is an important insight at a time when Western governments seem particularly eager to transform the public sector in order to improve its ability to deal efficiently, effectively and democratically with proliferating wicked and unruly problems (Levin et al. 2012), as well as to overcome growing legitimacy problems (Dalton 2004; Rothstein 2014).

The article starts by outlining the emerging public innovation agenda and its tendency to overlook political innovations. Political innovations are then defined, and their important role in public innovation is described. With a point of departure in cutting-edge public policy and governance research, I list a number of research themes and questions that call for studies of, and between, innovations in polity, politics and policy, and I assess the prospects for political innovation to rise to the top of the public sector innovation agenda in the coming years.

The emerging agenda on public sector innovation

Until recently, it was a truism that public bureaucracies were naturally, either for better or worse, resistant and aversive to change, and were capable of no creativity to speak of (Weber 1947; Downs 1957). Innovation was perceived as something businesses carried out in order to survive in competitive markets and, if anything, the role of the public sector was to give domestic firms easy access to innovation assets, such as cutting-edge scientific knowledge, a well-educated labour force, and a supportive infrastructure. The purpose was to spur economic growth and prosperity in society, and the private sector was perceived as the motor for achieving this (OECD 2015). A Google search for the terms 'public sector and innovation' illustrates that this approach to the relationship between the public sector and innovation still prevails, with triple helix and partnership models featuring among more recent developments in our understanding of how the public sector can promote private innovation and growth (Leydesdorff and Etzkowitz 1998; National Science Foundation 2015). However, a new public sector approach to innovation is gradually gaining momentum in Western liberal democracies, which focuses on how the public sector itself can become more innovative. In Canada, the government has set in motion an innovation process that aims to recast the public school system in order to focus on learning instead of teaching; Danish municipalities are currently engaged in developing services for the elderly that focus on rehabilitation rather than care; and the UK is on the lookout for new innovative measures to engage the public in ensuring public safety through different forms of community policing. What unites these endeavours is that they represent open-ended attempts to develop new, innovative approaches to solving public tasks.

Claims to causality are a risky business in the social sciences, and caution is called for when it comes to explaining why new issues enter government agendas. Robert Kingdon (1984) points to randomness, coincidence and policy entrepreneurs with a good sense of timing as important factors in agenda setting; and Christopher Pollitt and Peter Hupe (2011, 641) use the term 'magic concept' to describe topics, such as 'innovation' that have what it takes to attract broad-based attention from decision makers, notably a vague, fuzzy meaning and positive connotations. Yet none of these factors can explain why public innovation is entering government agendas right now. Innovation theory is helpful, however, in pointing out that innovations are driven by push and pull factors (Torfing 2016). Pull factors are when ambitions are voiced and appear realistic to pursue. Push factors are when a given state of affairs is perceived as dangerous and unsustainable.

Taking departure in this *pull-push terminology*, the growing interest in making the public sector more innovative can, on the pull factor side, be explained by positive experiences with introducing ICT in the public sector in the 1990s that have nurtured a growing belief in, and ambition to develop, a new and different kind of public sector (Contini and Anzara 2009). The push factors include: intensified global competition that has transformed nations into competition states (Cerny 1997). Whether a country wins or loses in the global competition for economic growth is no longer viewed as depending solely on the ability of domestic firms to innovate, and the support they get from public authorities in doing so. Winning or losing also depends on the efficiency and effectiveness of the way society is governed. Since the 1980s, governments have launched initiatives and reforms aimed at rendering public governance more efficient and effective (Hood 1991; Osborne and Gaebler 1993), but disappointing efficiency gains, growing fiscal austerity and rising citizen demands for public services at the beginning of the twenty-first century have put pressure on Western governments to find more radical ways to create more for less, and innovation promises exactly that (Pollitt 2010; Hood and Dixon 2015). In addition to the pressure for increased efficiency, there is a push to improve the quality of public governance. The public performance measurement regimes that emerged in the wake of the New Public Management reforms of the 1980s and 1990s have revealed an effectiveness deficit in a number of policy areas. The problem-solving capacity of the public sector is simply insufficient. Some researchers explain this effectiveness deficit as the result of a growth in wicked policy problems with a high level of complexity (Mayntz 1993; Kooiman 1993; Pierre and Peters 2000; Koppenjan and Klijn 2004); while others speak of policy execution problems stemming from misinformed policies (Macmillan and Cain 2010). The message is the same, however: the public sector must become more effective, and that calls for innovation.

After the turn of the century, many public policy and governance researchers parted ways with the general assumption that public innovation is an oxymoron, and embarked on open-ended studies of the realities of public sector innovation, developing theories that sought to identify the specific drivers and barriers to public innovation, and proposing ways to make the public sector more innovative (Borins 2001, 2014; Eggers and Singh 2009; Bekkers, Edelenbos, and Steijn 2011; Hartley, Sørensen, and Torfing 2013; Agger and Sørensen 2014; Ansell and Torfing 2015). The main focus of attention in this research has been on service innovation, for example, innovations in the content of public services as well as in the way they are provided. This service-oriented approach to innovation is inspired by traditional as well as newer theories of private sector innovation (Schumpeter 1939; Nijssen et al. 2006) that speak directly to the aspirations of current governments to develop a public sector that produces more and better public services for less.

The emerging research on public service innovation is important, but it tends to overlook the fact that, unlike in the private sector, public innovation takes place in a political-organizational context. Public service innovations are not only conditioned by what service users want but also by what political decision makers prioritize in terms of funding, and chose to regulate with reference to more or less contested political perceptions of what is right, just and valuable for the individual citizens as well as for society.

This political context has two immediate implications for a research agenda on public innovation. First, it calls for studies of how public service innovation is conditioned by existing policies and the political climate that exists in a given context. Studies are needed of service innovations in the light of whether or not they are developed in a context of intense political contestation. Also relevant are studies of how bottom-up service innovations initiated and developed by employees and/or relevant and affected citizens are endorsed by politicians, and of how, and to what effect, service innovations are initiated by governments as part of their political programmes.

Second, a comprehensive public innovation research programme must include studies of political innovations in their own right. Political institutions (polity), processes (politics) and programmes (policy) are more or less constantly being transformed, but these transformations are rarely analysed as instances of public innovation. Public innovation research must be able to provide descriptions, analyses and assessments of any resulting changes in the political system, as well as in their purpose and impact, including how the changes affect political systems' own ability to innovate in the years that follow. The proposed distinction between innovations in polity, politics and policy is intended for analytical purposes only, and a research agenda should not fail to include studies of how the three are interrelated. Institutional innovations may or may not promote innovations in politics, and innovations in politics may either reduce or hamper political systems' policy innovation capacity. A new, innovative policy may also affect political institutions in ways that promote or hamper future policy innovations. Hence, theory building and empirical research are needed that improve our knowledge about the interdependencies between innovations in polity, politics and policy (Agger and Sørensen 2014; Helms 2015). Figure 1 illustrates the types of innovations and interdependencies that lend themselves to theorizing and investigation as part of a research agenda on political innovation.

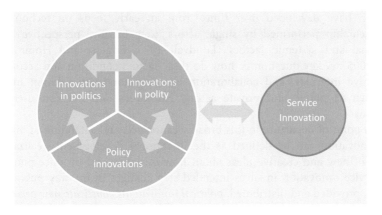

Figure 1. Research agenda on political innovation

What are innovations in polity, politics and policy?

The first step in clarifying what political innovation is must be to define innovation. Although definitions of innovation differ greatly, most innovation theories would agree that innovation involves *an intentional development and realization of new creative ideas* (Torfing 2016). Innovations can be new products but they can also be new organizational designs, and production methods and processes. In order to count as an innovation, the thing that is being developed must be qualitatively new and produce some form of qualitative step change, discontinuity or, as Schumpeter (1939) calls it, 'creative destruction' of existing products, structures or processes. The new thing does not have to qualify as 'never seen before' to count as an innovation, but must be new to the context in question, and innovations can be, and often are, adaptions of innovations developed elsewhere (Rogers 1995). The diffusion of innovations is therefore not only important because it secures the more extensive application of a new innovation, but also because diffusion tends to inspire and trigger innovations in other contexts. The same dynamic applies to innovations in products, structures and processes.

Innovations can take the form of small, incremental adjustments but they can also be radical in the sense that they turn things around completely, leading to a third order reconceptualization of the meaning and purpose of a phenomenon. All innovations involve risk taking (Osborne and Brown 2013), but radical innovations are particularly risky because the unintended outcomes that most innovations produce can be costly and difficult to remedy (Keizer and Halman 2007). Incremental, step-by-step innovations tend to result in fewer, and less devastating, failures and disasters, but the potential gains are also fewer. Although the term 'innovation' has positive connotations, innovations can also have negative outcomes, and appraisals about whether a concrete innovation is good or bad depends on who is doing the looking, and can vary considerably (Hartley 2005). Seen from the perspective of the innovators, an innovation is good if it meets their initial intentions, but other actors may disagree with those intentions or evaluate outcomes differently. In addition to the ever-present risk of failure, innovations are further complicated by the fact that the wish for innovations must in most cases be balanced against other goals, for example, the need for stability in political systems. Perceptions of what drives innovation have developed over time, from an early focus on technology and entrepreneurship performed by single actors, to a broader perspective involving institutional and systemic factors (Lundvall 1985; Edquist and Hommen 1999; Edquist 2005). A key question is: how do these factors condition and accommodate a productive interplay, and collaboration among actors with relevant innovation assets, such as public and private actors, employees and the end users of the innovations?

With a point of departure in this broadly canonized understanding of innovation, public innovation can be defined as the intentional development, realization and diffusion of new and creative ideas about how to define and produce public value. While service innovation involves intended step changes in the way public value is produced, provided and distributed, *political innovations constitute new perceptions of what counts as public value and new ways of transforming these perceptions into authoritative goals, principles and rules for public governance.* Implicit in this conceptualization is the idea that public sector innovations are always, more or less explicitly, conditioned by political factors. As such, political innovations are not only important in their own right, but also because they condition the scope for all other forms of public innovation. This 'primacy of the political' in public innovation has to do with the fact that what is perceived as non-political at a given point in time, for example, normalized perceptions of public purpose and routine ways of fulfilling that purpose in the form of existing public services, is a product of what Ernesto Laclau (1990) conceptualizes as hegemonic manifestations of past political battles which can be re-politicized at any point in time. Thus, for example, service innovations that are seemingly devoid of political implications can become re-politicized from one moment to the next. Political innovations and service innovations are thus intrinsically interlinked.

Political innovations can take three forms. *Innovations in polity* involve intentional efforts to reorganize external boundaries with other polities as well as the institutional framework, and procedures that regulate the formation and enactment of democratically authorized decisions about what counts as public value in a political community. *Innovations in politics* refer to the development and implementation of new ways for political actors to obtain democratically legitimate political power and influence. Finally, *innovations in policy* involve reformulations and elaborations of new political visions, goals, strategies and policy programmes that aim to guide the production of public value.

Research questions to be addressed

Political innovations are, then, arguably an overlooked research area, but is there really a need for this kind of research right now? With a point of departure in literature analysing current challenges to the political system in Western representative democracies, this section aims to show that there is, indeed, a pressing need for studies of the conditions for, and impact of, political innovations in and between polity, politics and policy. Moreover, it lists a number of research questions to be addressed in studies of the innovation capacity of the political system in contemporary representative democracies, and analyses how innovations in policy, politics and policy might enhance the innovation capacity of the public sector.

Innovations in polity

As mentioned above, the term 'polity' refers to spatially demarcated political units as well as to the institutional arrangements that regulate and authorize actors to govern a political community. A polity is both defined with reference to its external sovereignty vis-à-vis other polities, and its internal sovereignty – that is, the way it distributes power internally (Prokhovnik 2008). In modern Western societies, the polity is a nation state, and democratic institutions distribute authoritative power within that nation state. One of the big challenges of our time is what Bob Jessop (2004) calls the de-stratification of politics, referring to the fact that political decision-making is increasingly moving away from the national level of governance to subnational and transnational levels of governance. With regard to the latter, some researchers are turning their attention towards the potentials of large cities as institutionalized arenas for collective political action (Brenner 2004; Barber 2013). In relation to the former, the problem is that the traditional institutions of democracy are designed to distribute power within a polity and therefore cannot function adequately in transnational multi-polity policymaking arenas where authoritative power and sovereignty is distributed horizontally rather than concentrated hierarchically (Nye 2008; Sørensen 2012). Transnational political institutions and organizations do exist but they are rarely strong enough to secure the level of collective political action needed to mobilize a collective political response to problems, such as global warming, regional conflicts, refugee flows and natural disasters that call for political action. Decision makers, like public policy and governance researchers, are therefore intensely engaged in debating how transnational political institutions could be strengthened, what such institutions might look like and how to overcome the barriers that prevent them from being established.

A key issue currently under debate is whether it would be more beneficial to establish some sort of world government or to aim for a network-like transnational institutional political structure; while others debate whether it would be wiser to develop new political institutions or to build on the ones that already exist (Rosenau and Czempiel 1992; Crozier, Huntington, and Watanuki 1995; Ansell 2000; Bohman 2005; Zürn 2000; Keane 2009; Held and Koenig-Archibugi 2014). Despite differences in opinion regarding these difficult issues, it is generally agreed that there is a pressing need to develop democratic political institutions that can promote effective governance and a democratically just distribution of political power between actors on the transnational political scene (Heffe, Kickert, and Thomassen 2000; Slaughter 2001; Hajer 2003; Bache and Flinders 2004; Held and Koenig-Archibugi 2014). Among these questions are: how can political authority be distributed between transnational and national levels of governance? How can equal political influence for citizens be secured at transnational levels of governance? What procedures must be in place to ensure that political decisions made at different levels of governance are coordinated and aligned so that they do not undermine each other? How can political authorities engaged in multi-level policymaking be held to account, and how can blame avoidance among them be prevented (Scharpf 1999; Peters and Pierre 2004; Benz and Papadopoulos 2006)? These, and other complex questions related to the development of the institutional set-up of representative governance, are being intensely researched and analysed but they are rarely addressed from a public innovation perspective. We therefore know little about how current institutional changes, for example, the surge of a multi-level political system, are likely to affect the capacity of representative democracies to launch and implement innovative institutional reforms in the years to come (Helms 2015; Sørensen 2015), just as we know little about how those changes will affect institutional stability.

Innovations in politics

The term 'politics' refers to the process through which policymaking takes place in practice within a given set of political institutions. Recent literature that analyses political processes in representative democracies concludes that we are currently facing a disenchantment with representative democracy (Dalton 2004; Stoker 2006; Alonso, Keane, and Merkel 2011; Rosanvallon 2011). Political parties no longer represent specific classes or social groups with particular interests to be defended (Johnston 2005), and party politics increasingly appear irrelevant to citizens. The result is a drop in membership of political parties and in voter turnout at elections. Voters are less loyal to specific political parties and shop around. Some citizens are losing interest in politics altogether, while others are turning to extra-parliamentary forms of political participation in local communities or national or global social movements – all of which are forms of political participation that are detached from representative democracy (Norris 2011; Dalton 2015). Some researchers argue that the solution for representative democracy would be to engage in a concerted effort to involve citizens more actively in policymaking processes within political parties, from formulating political programmes to campaigning (Faucher-King 2005, 2015; Stoker 2006), forming new parties, and other supplementary forms of political participation in and around political assemblies and committees (Roberts and Bradley 1991; Hirst 2000; Warren 2002; Sørensen and Torfing 2005; Dalton 2015; Smith 2009; Michels 2011; Sørensen and Waldorff 2014). It is thought that closer dialogue between citizens and elected politicians will not only rekindle citizens' interest in politics but also ensure that the issues addressed by elected politicians and decision makers are perceived as relevant by the citizens themselves; that citizens' perspectives are brought to the table; and that the affected members of the political community feel a sense of ownership over the political visions, strategies and goals that are formulated and pursued in the political process. A much debated concern is whether this form of policymaking is too time consuming, and the extent to which the result will be an activist democracy that further empowers those who are already empowered at the cost of the political influence of citizens with fewer political capacities and competencies (Young 2000; Fung 2006; Hansen 2007).

Another prominent issue in current research on political processes in contemporary representative democracies is that the electoral cycle, as well as the political contestation and majoritarian system of representative party politics, tends to cultivate a short-term rather than a long-term perspective on policy outcomes (Pierson 2000; Jacobs 2011). The quest for voter support motivates political parties to choose political solutions that produce positive outcomes in the short term although other political measures would be more effective in the long run. Moreover, majority decisions that lead to large investments in achieving long-term results may be abandoned if elections lead to a shift in the political majority and thus a change in policies halfway through their implementation phase (Lees-Marshment 2014). Coalition building and the formation of broad inter-party alliances is proposed as a way of ensuring that a change in majority does not undermine long-term policy investments, and empirical analyses testify to a growth in inter-party coalitions (Baron and Ferejohn 1989; Laver and Shepsle 1995; Scharpf 1994; Martin and Stevenson 2001; Lees-Marshment 2011). Studies also show that the formation of broad alliances with strong, relevant and affected stakeholders enhances the sustainability of political reforms (Patashnik 2003). In addition, broad coalitions may make political parties more willing to go along with unpopular decisions.

The extensive research on developments in the political process in contemporary Western countries has identified important challenges to representative democracy and suggested possible means to overcome these challenges. Suggestions include the more active involvement of citizens at different stages of the policy process, and a move from majority rule to coalition building and negotiated politics that makes long-term collective political action possible in an otherwise strongly competitive political world of party and interest politics. However, research on these issues is mostly focused on analysing challenges to the democratic quality and effectiveness of the political process, while leaving unanswered questions related to the innovativeness of the political process itself. Studying these changes from an innovation perspective trains the lens on how new political practices affect the flexibility, as well as the solidity, of the political process.

Innovations in policy

Policy innovations are deliberate efforts to develop and promote new political visions, goals, strategies and policy programmes. All these aspects of a policy are important because they define public value and guide efforts to produce and distribute it. As documented in public policy and governance research, there is a permanent tension between political and administrative aspects of policy content (Peters 2001). While the formulation of political visions is clearly political, administrative aspects must also be considered when it comes to developing goals, strategies and policy programmes, whose realistic implementation depends not only on what is politically possible but also what is technically feasible in a given context. The growing awareness of the interrelatedness between political and administrative aspects of policy formulation among public policy and governance researchers has led to the broadly held conclusion that policies are, and should invariably be, co-productions between politicians and administrators (Kingdon 1984; Polsby 1984; Gray and Lowery 2000; Svara 1998, 2001).

The last thirty years of New Public Management and New Public Governance reforms have mainly aimed to de-bureaucratize public service delivery in order to render it more efficient and effective (Pollitt and Bouckaert 2004, 2012; Torfing et al. 2012; Osborne 2010), the goal being to strengthen the strategic leadership of public managers, and to introduce new governance techniques and tool kits, such as management by objectives, incentives steering, outsourcing, partnership formation and networks, user involvement, strategic management, performance measurement and process facilitation. Few reforms have aimed to enhance the political leadership and policy development capacity of elected politicians, however, and many researchers are worried that the content of public policies is becoming increasingly technocratic and weakly rooted in political visions, goals and strategies (Christensen and Lægreid 2007). Some researchers even talk about a depoliticization tendency where policies are motivated by references to the necessary and possible rather than to the normatively desirable and chosen (Wood 2015; Flinders and Wood 2015). Others point to the growing politicization of bureaucracy (Aucoin 2012). An emerging literature calls for policies based on politically anchored visions, goals and strategies, and posits a need to strengthen the political leadership of elected politicians, defined as their capacity to identify policy problems that call for collective political action, propose political strategies for solving them, and mobilize support and willingness to contribute to their implementation among members of the political community (Hartley 2005; Sørensen 2006; Koppenjan, Kars, and Voort 2009; Sørensen and Torfing 2016). Another body of literature claims that what is needed is the reinstatement of a public administration driven by professional values and norms rather than political tactics (Bakvis and Jarvis 2012). The shared ambition is to promote the balanced politico-administrative production of public policies that are politically motivated and guided by professional norms and standards. Although there are studies showing how recent government reforms have caused a shift in policy content – favouring efficiency and effectiveness over legality and public purpose – few studies have analysed how this change in focus has affected the political system's policy innovation capacity. Has it triggered creativity and enabled the prototyping of new policy ideas? Or has it narrowed the horizons of what it is possible and appropriate to propose in political programmes?

The interrelatedness between innovations in polity, politics and policy

As mentioned earlier, the distinction between innovations in polity, politics and policy is analytical rather than empirical. It helps to clarify that political innovations involve institutional change as well as changes in political processes and output, but we should not overlook the strong interrelatedness between the three forms of political innovation, which calls for research. Political institutions affect policy processes and policy outputs, and vice versa. Due to this interrelatedness, the rise of an increasingly multi-level political system will not only affect the capacity of representative democracies to redesign themselves in the years to come, but also their policy innovation capacity. What effect will this have? Will the growing institutional complexity enhance or reduce the ability of political actors at transnational, national and subnational levels to develop and pursue new policies? It is also relevant to consider how new forms of coalition building will affect the policy innovation capacity of political assemblies, and whether the involvement of citizens in policy processes will strengthen or weaken the capacity of political parties and political leaders to develop innovative political programmes. Moreover, the tendency to involve more actors in the political process may actually reduce or transform the role perceptions of the involved actors, and thus also their power in terms of political authority and legitimacy. Finally, new innovative policies can transform political processes and institutions. Most new policies involve a redistribution of responsibilities among public actors as well as among public and private actors and, in so doing, those policies also reshape the conditions for future political battles. Hence, policy reforms that decentralize service provision and political choice, and voice to local public and private actors and citizens affect political processes as well as institutional forms of representative democracy in ways that have implications for the political innovativeness of the public sector, as well as for its ability to initiate and monitor service innovation.

Different aspects of this interrelatedness among political innovations are being analysed in the other articles in this special issue. In 'Political innovation as ideal and strategy: the case of aleatoric democracy in the City of Utrecht', Albert Meijer, Reinout van der Veer, Albert Faber and Julia Penning de Vries analyse a new innovation in politics, for example, the use of lottery as a means to select participants in minipublics. The purpose of the study is to conceptualize and understand the interplay between idealist and realist drivers in at play in political innovations. The article aims to understand the role of idealism as well as strategy in politics, and show how these forces interact in a concrete political innovation process. Moreover, the article shows how the innovation in politics they call Aleatoric Democracy affects the larger functioning of the institutions of representative democracy.

In 'Strengthening political leadership and policy innovation through the expansion of collaborative forms of governance', Christopher Ansell and Jacob Torfing study the interrelatedness between political leadership, political processes and policy innovation. They aim to show how collaboration among politicians, citizens, and relevant and affected stakeholders can enhance the policy innovation capacity of representative democracy, thereby strengthening the political leadership of elected politicians. Illustrative examples from different levels of governance and different Western liberal states are provided that illuminate barriers to, as well as opportunities for, strengthening political leadership through new collaborative forms of policy innovation.

In their article, 'The challenge of innovating politics in community self-organization: the case of Broekpolder', Jurian Edelenbos, Ingmar van Meerkerk and Joop Koppenjan present an in-depth, longitudinal case study of a collaborative policy innovation process involving elected politicians and citizens. The study aims to show how the turn to self-governed forms of community-based policy innovation challenges traditional perceptions of what it means to be a politician, and seeks to clarify how politicians react and respond to this new way of organizing the political process. The study shows that the involved politicians have a hard time redefining their role as politicians in ways that allow them to participate in the policy innovation process in productive ways. In this unfamiliar situation, they fall back into a traditional politician role. As such, the study shows that the policy innovation capacity of self-governing communities depends on the extent to which it is possible for politicians to invent and grow accustomed to a new political leadership role.

Flemming Juul Christiansen and Carina Saxlund Bischoff seek to develop a theoretical framework for analysing innovations in political representation. In their article, 'Political parties and innovation', they look at political parties as agents of political representation and explore how current changes in their role and functioning can accommodate or hamper innovations in politics and policy. Their theoretical framework takes its point of departure in the idea that political parties are carriers of new (or old) political ideas, and explores how they promote or preclude the implementation of those ideas. The authors develop a typology for ideal typical dimensions of party representation, and these ideal types are then related to the concept of innovation. The value of applying the typology in analysing political parties is illustrated in a study of the 'The Alternative', a new innovative party that entered the Danish Parliament in 2015, and which has radically redefined what it means to represent the people.

Sarah Ayres' article explores the role of informal governance in creating and shaping political innovation. In her article, 'Assessing the impact of informal governance on political innovation', she argues that an analysis of informal governance is essential if we are to fully understand how political innovation occurs. In a case study of English devolution processes, she studies the impact of informal governance on innovations in polity (institutions), politics (process) and policy (outcomes). Defining informal governance as a means of decision-making that is un-codified, non-institutional and where social relationships play crucial roles, she concludes even when formal structures and procedures are weak, political innovation can still thrive if informal structures are in place that support such innovations.

Barriers to promoting a political innovation agenda

As described above, there are mounting challenges to the political system that make political innovations pertinent to the public innovation agenda. How can we then explain the limited interest among governments and public policy and governance researchers in pushing this agenda forward? Seen from the perspective of governments and other political actors, there is neither a lack of push nor pull factors that could trigger an interest in innovations in policy, politics and policy, and the interdependencies between them. The push factors include declining trust in elected politicians that undermines not only the legitimacy of the institutions of representative democracy, but also the authority of political leaders (Hetherington 2004).

Pull factors include the relentless competitive pressures on politicians to develop new, innovative political programmes and policy agendas to reshape political life in representative democracies (Kingdon 1984; Polsby 1984). However, these pull and push factors tend to be neutralized by institutional and procedural features within the political system itself (Rahat 2008). Paul Pierson (2000) calls these kinds of institutional neutralizations path dependencies or increasing returns, while Bob Jessop (1990) speaks of structural selectivity. Even though many politicians might desire substantial step changes in political institutions, the political process provides weak incentives, opportunities and motivation to invest in such an endeavour. Especially discouraging in that regard is the short political time frame dictated by electoral cycles (Pierson 2000). Moreover, politicians in office are rarely interested in changing the rules of the game that brought them into power, and their powerful position means that they can block change. When it comes to opposition parties and individual politicians, a political campaign aiming to improve the policy innovation capacity of the political system might mobilize some attention, but rarely enough to win elections. Another factor that could prevent politicians from addressing the need for innovations in the political process is that they sometimes prosper from its deficiencies. Hence, political deadlock and stalemate are not always perceived as problematic. Sometimes they function as attractive blame avoidance opportunities or as excuses for not acting (Weaver 1986). A final neutralization mechanism has to do with the generally high level of risk involved in innovating. The outcome of innovations is unpredictable and success is far from certain. The willingness to take risks to change the formal and informal conditions for policymaking is likely to be particularly low because the cost of rocking the boat could be detrimental and difficult to remedy due to the new political dynamics that result. What we face here is a typical collective action problem. Although a political system with a high polity, politics and policy innovation capacity may be in the collective long-term interest of elected politicians, none of them have an individual short-term interest in bringing this issue onto the political agenda. Research could play a role in reactivating existing pull and push factors through the production of knowledge about existing innovation barriers in the political system, through assessments of the risks and potential gains involved in political innovations, and through the prescription of ways to balance the need for innovation against the need for stability in political institutional arrangements, processes and policy contents.

Why, then, have political innovations remained a relatively unexplored research area? As described earlier, there are plenty of push factors in the form of well-documented and extensively researched deficiencies and limitations in existing political institutions, policy processes and policies in representative democracies. There is also evidence of how these deficiencies hamper the ability of elected politicians to find new ways to interact with citizens who want more influence than they get through the ballot box (Bang and Sørensen 1998; Dalton 2015; Norris 2011), to pursue new avenues in dealing with unruly policy problems, such as poverty, unemployment, lifestyle-related illnesses, public safety, financial bubbles, immigration and climate change (Levin et al. 2012), and to overcome the often detrimental political effects of mediatized party politics (Hindmoor 2008). Research is obviously needed that can bring new insights about how representative democracies can improve their capacity to innovate their own functioning. There are also pull factors in the form of research funding from the EU and other large-scale funding agencies, although this funding is more limited than when it comes to research on public service innovation. Publication opportunities are also beginning to emerge, and we are particularly grateful to *Public Management Review* for offering such opportunities.

The main barrier to putting political innovation on the public innovation research agenda seems to be disciplinary boundaries. Public innovation was originally developed as a part of a public administration research endeavour to make the public sector more efficient, and the focus was on the role of different forms of steering, managerial tool kits and ICT, and other technical innovations (Osborne and Gaebler 1993; Kraemer, Anderson, and Perry 1994). This disciplinary anchorage meant that political science issues received little attention. This disciplinary boundary between public administration and political science has prevented the public innovation agenda from spreading from service innovation to issues related to innovations in polity, politics and policy. As such, a research agenda on public innovation that addresses questions related to political innovations as well as service innovations calls for a cross-disciplinary research approach. A cross-disciplinary approach would help to prevent path dependencies in the social sciences that blind us to the interdependencies between politics and administration, and would enable the development of a coherent, systemic understanding of the conditions for public innovation, the interdependencies between political innovations and service innovations, and the relationship between institutional changes, process changes and policy and service content. This type of research approach would support the development of a theory of public innovation that takes full account of the differences as well as the similarities between public and private innovation.

Conclusion

This article set out to show that political innovations are an important field of study for public policy and governance scholars. The growing interest in promoting public innovation among Western governments has mainly focused on service innovations, as has the recent research on public innovation. While public service innovation is an important research area, I argue that political innovations are worthwhile objects of study in their own right. Public service innovations take place within political systems and cannot be fully comprehended without analysing how they are related to political innovations. Unlike private sector innovation research, a comprehensive public innovation research agenda must explore innovations in polity, politics and policy. I should recapitulate that neither service innovation nor political innovation are goals in themselves or even necessarily beneficial. At times, a stable public sector may seem more appealing than an innovative public sector. I have tried to show, however, that governments as well as researchers are currently struggling with problems and challenges that call not only for public service innovations but also for political innovations. This article has taken a first modest step towards developing a conceptual framework for studying political innovations, and listed some of the research themes to be addressed. There are institutional barriers in the public sector, as well as disciplinary boundaries in research, which seem to prevent political innovations from becoming an integrated part of the surging public sector innovation agenda. I hope that this article, as well as the other articles in this special issue, will inspire other researchers to join forces in this important endeavour.

Disclosure statement

No potential conflict of interest was reported by the authors.

References

Agger, A., and E. Sørensen. 2014. "Designing Collaborative Policy Innovation: Lessons from a Danish Municipality." In *Public Innovation through Collaboration and Design*, edited by C. Ansell and J. Torfing, 188–208. New York: Routledge.

Alonso, S., J. Keane, and W. Merkel. 2011. *The Future of Representative Democracy*. Cambridge: Cambridge University Press.

Ansell, C. 2000. "The Networked Polity: Regional Development in Western Europe." *Governance* 13 (2): 279–291. doi:10.1111/gove.2000.13.issue-2.

Ansell, C., and J. Torfing. 2015. "How Does Collaborative Governance Scale?" *Policy & Politics* 43 (3): 315–329. doi:10.1332/030557315X14353344872935.

Aucoin, P. 2012. "New Political Governance in Westminster Systems: Impartial Public Administration and Management Performance at Risk." *Governance* 25 (2): 177–199. doi:10.1111/gove.2012.25.issue-2.
Bache, I., and M. Flinders, eds. 2004. *Multi-level Governance*. Oxford: Oxford University Press.
Bakvis, H., and M. D. Jarvis, eds. 2012. *From New Public Management to New Political Governance*. Montreal: McGill University Press.
Bang, H. P., and E. Sørensen. 1998. "The Everyday Maker: A New Challenge to Democratic Governance." *Administrative Theory & Praxis* 21 (3): 325–341. doi:10.1080/10841806.1999.11643381.
Barber, B. 2013. *If Mayors Ruled the World: Dysfunctional Nations, Rising Cities*. New Haven, CT: Yale University Press.
Baron, D. P., and J. A. Ferejohn. 1989. "Bargaining in Legislatures." *The American Political Science Review* 83 (4): 1181–1206. doi:10.2307/1961664.
Bekkers, V., J. Edelenbos, and B. Steijn, eds. 2011. *Innovation in the Public Sector. Linking Capacity and Leadership*. Basingstoke: Palgrave Macmillan.
Benz, A., and Y. Papadopoulos, eds. 2006. *Governance and Democracy*. London: Routledge.
Bohman, J. 2005. "From Demos to Demoi: Democracy Across Borders." *Ratio Juris* 18 (3): 293–314. doi:10.1111/raju.2005.18.issue-3.
Borins, S. 2001. "Encouraging Innovation in the Public Sector." *Journal of Intellectual* 2 (3): 310–319.
Borins, S. 2014. *The Persistence of Innovation in Government: A Guide for Innovative Public Servants*. Innovation Series. Boston, MA: IBM Centre for Business of Government.
Brenner, N. 2004. *New State Spaces: Urban Governance and the Rescaling of Statehood*. Oxford: Oxford University Press.
Cerny, P. G. 1997. "Paradoxes of the Competition State: The Dynamics of Political Globalization." *Government and Opposition* 32 (2): 251–274. doi:10.1111/j.1477-7053.1997.tb00161.x.
Christensen, T., and P. Lægreid. 2007. *Transcending New Public Management: The Transformation of Public Sector Reforms*. Aldershot: Ashgate.
Contini, F., and G. F. Anzara, eds. 2009. *ICT and Innovation in the Public Sector: European Studies in the Making of E-Government*. Basingstoke: Palgrave Macmillan.
Crozier, M., S. P. Huntington, and J. Watanuki. 1995. *'The Crisis of Democracy: On the Governability of Democracies', Trilateral Commission Report*. New York: New York University Press.
Dalton, R. J. 2004. *Democratic Challenges, Democratic Choices: The Erosion of Political Support in Advanced Industrial Democracies*. Oxford: Oxford University Press.
Dalton, R. J. 2015. *The Good Citizen. How a Younger Generation in Reshaping American Politics*. Los Angeles, CA: Sage.
Downs, A. 1957. *An Economic Theory of Democracy*. New York: Harper.
Edquist, C. 2005. "Systems of Innovation: Perspectives and Challenges." In *Oxford Handbook of Innovation*, edited by J. Fagerberg, D. Mowery, and R. Nelson, 181–208. Oxford: Oxford University Press.
Edquist, C., and L. Hommen. 1999. "Systems of Innovation: Theory and Policy for the Demand Side." *Technology in Society* 21 (1): 63–79. doi:10.1016/S0160-791X(98)00037-2.
Eggers, B., and S. Singh. 2009. *The Public Innovators Playbook*. Washington, DC: Harvard Kennedy School of Government.
EU-Commission. 2013. *Powering European Public Sector Innovation: Towards a New Architecture*. Report of the Expert Group on public sector innovation, EUR 13825 EN. Brussels: EU-Commission.
Faucher-King, F. 2005. *Changing Parties: An Anthropology of British Political Party Conferences*. Basingstoke: Palgrave Macmillan.
Faucher-King, F. 2015. "New Forms of Political Participation. Changing Demands or Changing Opportunities to Participate in Political Parties?" *Comparative European Politics* 13 (4): 405–429. doi:10.1057/cep.2013.31.
Flinders, M., and M. Wood, eds. 2015. *Depoliticisation, Governance and the State*. Bristol: Polity Press.
Fung, A. 2006. *Empowered Participation: Reinventing Urban Democracy*. Princeton: Princeton University Press.

Gray, V., and D. Lowery. 2000. "Where Do Policy Ideas Come from? A Study of Minnesota Legislators and Staffers." *Journal of Public Administration Research Theory* 10 (3): 573–598. doi:10.1093/oxfordjournals.jpart.a024282.

Hajer, M. 2003. "Policy without Polity? Policy and the Institutional Void." *Policy Sciences* 36 (2): 175–195. doi:10.1023/A:1024834510939.

Hansen, A. D. 2007. "Governance Networks and Participation." In *Theories of Democratic Network Governance*, edited by E. Sørensen and J. Torfing, 249–260. London: Palgrave Macmillan.

Hartley, J. 2005. "Innovation in Governance and Public Service: Past and Present." *Public Money & Management* 25 (1): 27–34.

Hartley, J., E. Sørensen, and J. Torfing. 2013. "Collaborative Innovation: A Viable Alternative to Market Competition and Organizational Entrepreneurship." *Public Administration Review* 73 (6): 821–830. doi:10.1111/puar.2013.73.issue-6.

Heffe, V. O., W. J. M. Kickert, and J. A. Thomassen, eds. 2000. *Governance in Modern Society: Effects, Change and Formation of Government Institutions.* Dordrecht: Kluwer Academic Publishers.

Held, D., and M. Koenig-Archibugi. 2014. *Global Policy: Power, Governance and Accountability.* Cambridge: Polity Press.

Helms, L. 2015. "Democracy and Innovation: From Institutions to Agency and Leadership." *Democratization.* http://www.tandfonline.com/doi/abs/10.1080/13510347.2014.981667#.VOYFQ010zLk

Hetherington, M. J. 2004. *Why Trust Matters: Declining Political Trust and the Demise of American Liberalism.* Princeton: Princeton University Press.

Hindmoor, A. 2008. "Policy Innovation and the Dynamics of Party Competition: A Schumpeterian Account of British Electoral Politics' 1950-2005." *Bjpir* 10 (3): 492–508.

Hirst, P. 2000. "Democracy and Governance." In *Debating Governance*, edited by J. Pierre, 13–36. Oxford: Oxford University Press.

Hood, C. 1991. "A Public Management for All Seasons?" *Public Administration* 69 (1): 3–19. doi:10.1111/padm.1991.69.issue-1.

Hood, C., and R. Dixon. 2015. *A Government that Worked Better and Cost Less? Evaluating Three Decades of Government Reform and Change in UK Central Government.* Oxford: Oxford University Press.

Jacobs, A. M. 2011. *Governing for the Long Run: Democracy and the Politics of Investment.* Cambridge: Cambridge University Press.

Jessop, B. 1990. *State Theory: Putting Capitalist States in their Place.* Cambridge: Polity Press.

Jessop, B. 2004. "Multi-Level Governance and Multi-Level Metagoverance." In *Multi-level Governance*, edited by I. Bache and M. Flinders, 49–74. Oxford: Oxford University Press.

Johnston, M. 2005. *Political Parties and Democracy in Theoretical and Practical Perspective.* Report for National Democratic Institute for International Affairs (NDI). Washington, DC: NDI (National Democratic Institute).

Keane, J. 2009. *The Life and Death of Liberal Democracy.* London: Simon & Schuster.

Keizer, J., and J. I. M. Halman. 2007. "Diagnosing Risk in Radical Innovation Projects." Research Technology Management. http://www.researchgate.net/publication/232274080

Kingdon, R. 1984. *Agendas, Alternatives, and Public Policies.* Boston: Little Brown.

Kooiman, J. 1993. *Modern Governance: New Government Society Interactions.* London: Sage.

Koppenjan, J., M. Kars, and H. V. D. Voort. 2009. "Vertical Politics in Horizontal Policy Networks: Framework Setting as Coupling Arrangements." *The Policy Studies Journal* 37 (4): 769–792. doi:10.1111/j.1541-0072.2009.00334.x.

Koppenjan, J., and E.-H. Klijn. 2004. *Managing Uncertainties in Networks.* London: Routledge.

Kraemer, K., K. V. Anderson, and J. L. Perry. 1994. "Information Technology and Transitions in the Public Service: A Comparison of Scandinavia and the United States." *International Journal of Public Administration* 17 (10): 1871–1905.

Laclau, E. 1990. *New Reflections on the Revolution of Our Time.* London: Verso.

Laver, M., and K. A. Shepsle. 1995. *Making and Breaking Governments: Cabinets and Legitimacy in Parliamentary Democracies'.* Cambridge: Cambridge University Press.

Lees-Marshment, J. 2011. *The Political Marketing Game.* Basingstoke: Palgrave Macmillan.

Lees-Marshment, J. 2014. *The Ministry of Public Input: Report and Recommendations for Practice.* Auckland: University of Auckland.

Levin, K., B. Cashore, S. Bernstein, and G. Auld. 2012. "Overcoming the Tragedy of Super Wicked Problems: Constraining our Future Selves to Ameliorate Global Climate Change." *Policy Sciences* 45 (2): 123–152. doi:10.1007/s11077-012-9151-0.

Leydesdorff, L., and H. Etzkowitz. 1998. "The Triple Helix as a Model for Innovation Studies'." *Science and Public Policy* 25 (3): 195–203.

Lundvall, B. Å. 1985. *Product Innovation and User-producer Interaction*. Aalborg: Aalborg University Press.

Macmillan, P., and T. Cain. 2010. *Closing the Gap: Eliminating the Disconnect Between Policy Design and Execution*. Vancouver: Deloitte.

Martin, L. W., and R. T. Stevenson. 2001. "Government Formation in Parliamentary Democracies." *American Journal of Political Science* 45: 33–50.

Mayntz, R. 1993. "Governing Failure and the Problem of Governability: Some Comments on a Theoretical Paradigm." In *Modern Governance*, edited by J. Kooiman, 9–20. London: Sage.

Michels, A. 2011. "Innovations in Democratic Governance: How Does Citizen Participation Contribute to a Better Democracy?" *International Review of Administrative Sciences* 77 (2): 275–293. doi:10.1177/0020852311399851.

Mulgan, J. 2014. "Innovation in the Public Sector: How can Public Organizations Better Create, Improve and Adapt." *NESTA*. UK-Governments Innovation Foundation. November 2014. http://www.nesta.org.uk/sites/default/files/innovation_in_the_public_sector-_how_can_public_organisations_better_create_improve_and_adapt.pdf

National Science Foundation. 2015. "Partnerships for Innovation." *PFI-program*. National Science foundation. http://www.nsf.gov/funding/pgm_summ.jsp?pims_id=5261

Nijssen, E. J., B. Hillebrand, P. Vermeulen, and R. Kemp. 2006. "Exploring Product and Service Innovation Similarities and Differences." *International Journal of Research in Marketing* 23 (3): 241–251. doi:10.1016/j.ijresmar.2006.02.001.

Norris, P. 2011. *Democratic Deficit: Critical Citizens Revisited*. Cambridge: Cambridge University Press.

Nye, J. 2008. *The Powers to Lead*. Oxford: Oxford University Press.

OECD. 2012. *Public-sector innovation', OECDs Science, Technology and Industry Outlook*. Paris: OECD Publishing. doi:10.1787/sti_outlook-2012-18-en.

OECD. 2015. *Innovation Policies for Inclusive Growth*. Paris: OECD Publishing. doi:10.1787/9789264229488-en.

Osborne, D., and T. Gaebler. 1993. *Reinventing Government: How the Entrepreneurial Spirit is Transforming the Public Sector*. Reading, MA: Addison-Wesley.

Osborne, S., ed. 2010. *The New Public Governance?* New York: Routledge.

Osborne, S. P., and K. Brown, eds. 2005. *Managing Change and Innovation in Public Service Organizations*. New York: Routledge.

Osborne, S. P., and L. Brown, eds. 2013. *Handbook of Innovations in Public Services*. Cheltenham: Edward Elgar.

Patashnik, E. 2003. "After the Public Interest Prevails: The Political Sustainability of Policy Reform." *Governance* 16 (2): 203–234. doi:10.1111/gove.2003.16.issue-2.

Peters, B. G., and J. Pierre. 2004. "Multi-level Governance and Democracy: A Faustian Bargin." In *Muliti-level Governance*, edited by I. Bache and M. Flinders. Oxford: Oxford University Press.

Peters, B. G. 2001. *The Politics of Bureaucracy*. Londong: Routledge.

Pierre, J., and B. G. Peters. 2000. *Governance, Politics and the State*. Basingstoke: Palgrave Macmillan.

Pierson, P. 2000. "Increasing Returns, Path-Dependence, and the Study of Politics." *The American Political Science Review* 94 (2): 251–267. doi:10.2307/2586011.

Pollitt, C. 2010. *Public Sector Reforms During Financial Austerity. Report to the Swedish Government*. Stockholm: Statskontoret.

Pollitt, C., and G. Bouckaert. 2004. *Public Management Reforms*. Oxford: Oxford University Press.

Pollitt, C., and G. Bouckaert. 2012. "Public Management Reform: A Comparative Analysis – New Public Management, Governance, and the Neo-Weberian State." *International Review of Administrative Sciences* 78 (1): 180–182. doi:10.1177/0020852312437323.

Pollitt, C., and P. Hupe. 2011. "Talking About Government." *Public Management Review* 13 (5): 641–658. doi:10.1080/14719037.2010.532963.

Polsby, N. W. 1984. *Political Institutions in America: The Politics of Policy Initiation*. New Haven, CT: Yale University Press.

Prokhovnik, R. 2008. *Sovereignty: History and Theory, Exeter*. Charlottesville, VA: Imprint Academic.

Rahat, G. 2008. *The Politics of Regime Structure Change in Democracies: Israel in Comparative and Theoretical Perspective*. New York: State University of New York Press.

Roberts, N., and R. T. Bradley. 1991. "Stakeholder Collaboration and Innovation: A Study of Public Policy Initiation at the State Level." *The Journal of Applied Behavioral Science* 27 (2): 209–227. doi:10.1177/0021886391272004.

Rogers, E. 1995. *Diffusion of Innovations*. New York: Free Press.

Rosanvallon, P. 2011. *Democratic Legitimacy. Impartiality, Reflexivity, Proximity*. Princeton: Princeton University Press.

Rosenau, J. N., and E.-O. Czempiel, eds. 1992. *Governance Without Government: Order and Change in World Politics*. Cambridge: Cambridge University Press.

Rothstein, B. 2014. "Political Legitimacy for Public Administration." In *The Sage Handbook of Public Administration*, 2nd ed., edited by B. G. Peters and J. Pierre, 357–369. London: Sage.

Scharpf, F. W. 1994. "Games Real Actors Could Play: Positive and Negative Coordination in Embedded Negotiations." *Journal of Theoretical Politics* 6 (1): 27–53. doi:10.1177/0951692894006001002.

Scharpf, F. 1999. *Governing in Europe: Effective and Democratic?* Oxford: Oxford University Press.

Schumpeter, J. 1939. *Business Circles: A Theoretical, Historical and Statistical Analysis of the Capitalist Process*. New York: McGraw Hill.

Slaughter, A. M. 2001. *Global Government Networks, Global Information Agencies, and Disintegrated Democracy*. Public Law Working Paper, no. 18. Boston, MA: Harvard Law School.

Smith, G. 2009. *Democratic Innovations*. Cambridge: Cambridge University Press.

Sørensen, E. 2006. "Metagovernance: The Changing Role of Politicians in Processes of Democratic Governance." *The American Review of Public Administration* 36 (1): 98–114. doi:10.1177/0275074005282584.

Sørensen, E. 2012. "Governance Networks as a Frame for Inter-Demoi Participation and Deliberation." *Administrative Theory & Praxis* 34 (4): 509–532. doi:10.2753/ATP1084-1806340401.

Sørensen, E. 2015. "Enhancing Policy Innovation by Redesigning Representative Democracy". *Politics & Policy*. http://www.ingentaconnect.com/content/tpp/pap/pre-prints/content-PP_072;jsessionid=1vank6pcmdsqp.alice

Sørensen, E., and J. Torfing. 2005. "The Democratic Anchorage of Governance Networks." *Scandinavian Political Studies* 28 (3): 195–218. doi:10.1111/scps.2005.28.issue-3.

Sørensen, E., and J. Torfing. 2016. "Political Leadership in the Age of Interactive Governance: Reflections on the Political Aspects of Metagovernance." In *Critical Reflections on Interactive Governance*, edited by J. Edelenbos and I. F. Meerkerk. Cheltenham: Edward Elgar.

Sørensen, E., and S. B. Waldorff. 2014. "Collaborative Policy Innovation." *The Innovation Journal* 19 (3): article 2. http://www.innovation.cc/scholarly-style/19_3_3_amdam_integrated-plan-learn452m.pdf

Stoker, G. 2006. *Why Politics Matter: Making Democracy Work*. Basingstoke: Palgrave Macmillan.

Svara, J. H. 1998. "The Politics-Administration Dichotomy Model as Aberration." *Public Administration Review* 58 (1): 51–58. doi:10.2307/976889.

Svara, J. H. 2001. "The Myth of the Dichotomy: Complementarity of Politics and Administration in the Past and Future of Public Administration." *Public Administration Review* 61 (2): 176–183. doi:10.1111/puar.2001.61.issue-2.

Torfing, J. 2016. *Collaborative Innovation in the Public Sector*. Washington: Georgetown University Press.

Torfing, J., B. G. Peters, J. Pierre, and E. Sørensen. 2012. *Interactive Governance: Advancing the Paradigm*. Oxford: Oxford University Press.

UK-Government. 2014. "Open Public Services 2014." *Policy Paper*. Cabinet Office, UK-GOV. https://www.gov.uk/government/publications/open-public-services-2014-progress-report/open-public-services-2014

US-Government. 2012. "Regulations.Gov: Remaking Public Participation." *The Open Government Partnership*. http://www.whitehouse.gov/blog/2012/02/21/regulationsgov-remaking-public-participation
US-Government. 2013. "The Second Open Government Action Plan." *US-Government*. Accessed 5 December 2013. What can democratic participation mean today? http://www.opengovpartnership.org/sites/default/files/US%20National%20Action%20Plan.pdf
Warren, M. E. 2002. "What Can Democratic Participation Mean Today?" *Political Theory* 30 (5): 677–701. doi:10.1177/0090591702030005003.
Weaver, R. K. 1986. "The Politics of Blame Avoidance." *Journal of Public Policy* 6 (4): 371–398. doi:10.1017/S0143814X00004219.
Weber, M. 1947. *The Theory of Social and Economic Organization*. Translated by A.M. Henderson and Talcott Parsons. London: Collier Macmillan Publishers.
Wood, M. 2015. "Politicisation, Depoliticisation and Antipolitics: Towards a Multilevel Research Agenda." *Political Studies Review*. doi:10.1111/1478-9302.12074.
Young, I. M. 2000. *Inclusion and Democracy*. Cambridge: Cambridge University Press.
Zürn, M. 2000. "Democratic Governance Beyond the Nation-State." In *Themocracy Beyond the State?* edited by M. T. Greven and L. W. Pauly, 91–114. Boston, MA: Rowman and Littlefield Publishers.

ⓐ OPEN ACCESS

Political innovation as ideal and strategy: the case of aleatoric democracy in the City of Utrecht

Albert Meijer, Reinout van der Veer, Albert Faber and Julia Penning de Vries

ABSTRACT
Political innovations aim to strengthen democracy but few connect well to the institutionalized democratic context. This paper explores how political innovations can be successfully embedded in existing democratic systems. It builds upon both the literature on political innovation and on new democratic arrangements and studies a practice of aleatoric democracy – using the lottery instead of elections to select representatives – in the Dutch City of Utrecht. The case study shows how the idealist logic of improving democracy and the realist logic of realizing specific political goals intertwine to get the political innovation accepted by the institutionalized democratic system.

Introduction

Models of representative democracy have proved to be remarkably stable in European and North American countries. Alternatives such as direct democracy have been propagated but they have never been able to overthrow the dominant model of choosing parliamentary and executive representatives to act for the people. This does not mean that these alternatives had no effect. Pleas for more direct citizen engagement have resulted in various amendments in the forms of hearings, referendums, public debates etc. These amendments can be regarded as processes of political innovation: new ideas are used to strengthen democracy (Smith 2009; Michels 2011). Not only lack of faith in existing representation but also the disintegration of civil society (Putnam 2000) explains the search for new forms of citizen engagement, and therefore, political innovation is high on the agenda of local governments around the world.

Many new democratic arrangements have been proposed but only few of them obtain a serious position in the institutionalized democratic context (Michels 2011). Innovations are often regarded as competitors rather than allies. Under what conditions are certain political innovations successfully connected to democratic systems that have existed for a long time? This paper aims to enhance our understanding of these processes of political innovation by analysing a specific amendment to western democratic models: the aleatoric democracy (Dowlen 2008). Aleatoric democracy

This is an Open Access article distributed under the terms of the Creative Commons Attribution-NonCommercial-NoDerivatives License (http://creativecommons.org/licenses/by-nc-nd/4.0/), which permits non-commercial re-use, distribution, and reproduction in any medium, provided the original work is properly cited, and is not altered, transformed, or built upon in any way.

means that representatives of the people are randomly selected through a lottery, they engage in collaborative decision-making and they are generally remunerated for their engagement. This form of democracy was the foundation of the ancient Greek polis of Athens and recently this idea is receiving new attention. It is presented as an important addition to existing democratic system and is also often referred to as 'mini-publics' (Goodin and Dryzek 2006; Smith 2009; Hendriks and Michels 2011). Our research enhances our understanding of the political innovation of local democracy by analysing this specific democratic arrangement.

This paper builds upon both theories of democracy (Pateman 1970; Barber 1984; Dahl 1998; Dryzek 2000; Fishkin 2009), theories of public innovation (Osborne and Brown 2005; Sørensen and Torfing 2011; Bekkers, Edelenbos, and Steijn 2011) and specific literature on democratic innovation (Smith 2009; Michels 2011). It develops a conceptual understanding of aleatoric democracy and analyses it as a political innovation and our analysis focuses on the different phases of the process of political innovation. Our theoretical framing of the connection between innovation and institutional context focuses on two classic political logics: an idealistic one in line with political philosophers such as Montesquieu, Rousseau, Mill and many others and a realist one that originates from Machiavelli, Von Clausewitz and, again, many others. Our analysis highlights how these two different logics of political innovation – an idealist logic and a strategic logic – are intertwined and generate the motivation and support for this political innovation.

The empirical material presented in this paper is a rich and detailed case of aleatoric democracy in the City of Utrecht in the Netherlands. The key feature of this process of political innovation is that citizens were randomly selected to participate, they received remuneration for their participation and they could be regarded as an alternative form of citizen representation. In contrast with many other forms of participation such as citizen panels, the advice was not 'free': local government had committed beforehand to follow this advice and to translate it to an energy policy plan. Our empirical analysis of this case shows that an interplay between idealist and realist logics explains why they are 'accepted' by the institutionalized democratic system.

Aleatoric democracy

The current system of representative democracy with a key role for the electoral process is both firmly established in Western democracies and heavily criticized. Criticists highlight that the system suffers from a lack of legitimacy and effectiveness and may result in an electoral aristocracy rather than popular rule (van Reybrouck 2013, 84). Corruption and a focus on limited and short-term interests are presented as the inevitable by-products of this arrangement and therefore radical changes are needed. This is an extensive debate that cannot be summarized in a few sentences but we will sketch the broad outlines of this debate to position aleatoric democracy as a political innovation.

The right to elect our rulers is seen as a cornerstone of democracy but representatives are often criticized for focusing on their own interests and failing to connect to the populace. The call for democratic innovation often relates to concerns on how to deal with so-called wicked problems (Rittel and Webber 1973). These are problems such as sustainability and urban safety that are not only complicated in terms of the knowledge needed to comprehend the problem and possible solutions but that are also challenging for the different value orientations. For this reason, new forms of politics may be needed to find collective solutions to these problems. Building upon a Habermassian notion of a public debate, interactive policymaking and other forms of citizen engagement have been propagated and implemented to strengthen democracy. Goodin and Dryzek (2006) identify citizen juries, consensus conferences and deliberative polls as new forms of engaging a 'mini-public' in the democratic process. A latest – but also an old – contribution to this debate is the idea of an aleatoric democracy. The key idea of an aleatoric democracy is that, similar to court juries in many countries, all citizens can be randomly selected to engage in collective decision-making processes. In ancient Athens, this meant that every year citizens were selected by drawing lots to rule the polis. This classic idea has been translated to our modern times and it is presented as a solution for the problems of democracy (Carson and Martin 1999). The selected citizens often receive a pay, are informed by experts and do not only deliberate options but actually develop laws and plans for the community (Smith 2009).

The idea of an aleatoric democracy combines some of the elements of other democratic systems. It engages a *representative group of citizens* in debates and decision-making. The difference with the electoral system is that the participants – representatives – are not elected but selected by drawing lots. In addition, it is a system for organizing the *political debate*. The fact that this debate takes place among a selected group of citizens not only limits the contributions but also facilitates consensus-seeking behaviour and mutual learning. While monitorial citizens (Schudson 1999) are motivated by private interests or a specific public interest and focus on critiquing government initiatives and actions, citizens in aleatoric democracy are expected to have a broader perspective on the public good and to be willing to co-produce decisions with government.

The contribution of aleatoric democracy can be assessed in terms of fairness and competence (Renn and Webler 1995). Fairness is a normative–ethical criterion which highlights that a process is fair if all participants have equal opportunities to influence the agenda and rules, equal opportunities to name the moderator and equal opportunities to participate in the debate (Webler 1995). Competence is a functional–analytical criterion that highlights that the process should offer the participants optimal opportunities to use available knowledge for the decision. Specifically, this means that the process should acknowledge and tap into the available knowledge and it should contain procedures for dealing with conflicts in knowledge claims.

Aleatoric democracy is heavily debated and there are both proponents and opponents of this system. Proponents highlight its capacity to advance public decision-making about wicked issues and to enhance citizen engagement (van Reybrouck 2013). We will not engage in the normative debate on aleatoric democracy but conduct an empirical analysis. In this paper, we conceptualize aleatoric democracy as a political innovation and analyse why this idea in a certain context is presented as a solution to democratic problems and how the political innovation is implemented and connects to the existing democratic institutions.

Political innovation

Political innovation as ideal and strategy

Change to political systems has been one of the key domains of research in the political sciences. Many interesting studies of political innovation have been published recently ranging from the stages of political innovation in rural China's local democratization (Zhang 2012) to the birth of a unique democracy in Karnataka (Raghavan and Manor 2012) and renewable energy in Australia (Effendi and Courvisanos 2012). Although some of these studies refer to the role of politics in developing innovative solutions to societal problems, most studies conceptualize political innovation as substantial changes to the political system motivated by new ideas about politics. Although theoretically the concept of political innovation could refer to new forms of authoritarian government, most research focuses on changes in democratic systems. For this reason, the words that are used to describe these political innovations range from democratic innovation (Smith 2009), innovation in democratic governance (Michels 2011) to deliberative innovations (Goodin and Dryzek 2006) and innovative democratic techniques (Goodin and Dryzek 2006).

Following Walker's (1969) classic discussion of the diffusion of innovation among American states, we define political innovation as a political mechanism, structure or process that is new to the specific polity. Similarly, Sørensen and Torfing (2011, 849) define innovation as the 'intentional and proactive process that involves the generation and practical adoption and spread of new and creative ideas, which aim to produce a qualitative change in a specific context'. This clearly underlines that it does not matter whether the approach has already been introduced elsewhere: it should be new in this context. The definition also stipulates that it is not a quantitative change – for example: more frequent elections – but a qualitative change: doing things differently. These two elements – 'newness' and 'qualitative change' – are (inter) subjective and therefore whether a change is seen as an innovation differs. Whether aleatoric democracy is perceived as a political innovation therefore needs to be investigated empirically.

Political innovation is defined 'intentional efforts to transform political institutions designed to make authorative political decisions (polity), the political processes that lead to such decisions (politics) and the content of the resulting policies (policy)' (Sørensen, 2016). They can be seen as a specific sort of institutional innovation in the sense that the rules which apply to the political process are changed – innovated – to produce more desirable outcomes (Bekkers, Edelenbos, and Steijn 2011). Political innovations can be analysed both as ideals in the sense that they aim to strengthen democratic quality and as strategies for realizing certain interests (cf. Stone 1997). Important changes in our electoral system such as right to vote for poor people, women and blacks not only have an idealist logic in the sense that they embody the empowerment of these groups but also a strategic component in these sense that certain political parties benefited from these changes in the electorate.

The *idealist logic* positions political innovation in the long tradition of the development of arrangements for dealing with disputes and value plurality in democratic society. This logic builds on a long intellectual tradition in political philosophy that started in ancient Greece with Plato's The Republic and that continued in the Age of Enlightenment with philosophers such as Montesquieu, Rousseau and Locke. The idealist logic stipulates how new ideas can strengthen our democratic systems (Dahl 1998). Ideas are formulated on the basis of different conceptions of what a democratic community entails and what should be seen as proper arrangements for dealing with conflict and allocation of scarce resources.

At the same time, however, this political innovation emerges at a specific place and a specific moment in time. This raises the question who finds the political innovation desirable and who manages to actually transform the idea into a practice. This means that the term 'political' in the term 'political innovation' does not only refer to the rules of the political game but also to the political – or strategic – motives for changing the rules of the game (Hix and Høyland 2011). In a *realist logic*, changing politics is political: new mechanisms are used to realize the outcomes that a specific actor or group finds desirable. This logic is rather different from the idealist logic that focuses on the nature of ideas and shifts the emphasis to the actual realization.

Phases in the process of political innovation

The analyses of political innovation generally build upon the seminal work of Rogers (1995). His work is used to study how and when innovation is adopted and how they disseminate over a larger population of nation states, states, provinces or local government. The process of innovation can be studied in terms of the different phases. Although these phase models have been criticized for being too sterile and not describing the messiness of actual innovation processes, their analytical value is broadly acknowledged. At the same time, the phase models need to be adapted to work for institutional changes such as political innovation. For this reason, we propose the following phase model for political innovation (cf. Osborne and Brown 2005, 129; Meijer 2014): (1) selecting the political innovation, (2) implementing the political innovation and (3) connecting the political innovation to the institutional context. These different phases can be used to analyse the adoption of the innovation, the implementation and its nexus to existing institutional structures. We will develop these phases further on the basis of the academic literature.

Ad 1. Selecting the political innovation

An idea to innovate politics has to compete with other promising ideas for support and (financial) resources (Morabito 2008). The classic approach to the adoption of innovation highlights that the uptake depends on two factors: perceived usefulness and barriers to adoption such as cost (Rogers 1995). The basic idea is that individuals will be more likely to adopt the innovation if they are aware of its value, see how it could be helpful to them in their specific context and consider the barriers to be limited. For political systems, this means that key actors have to be able to frame the political innovation as useful and the barriers as surmountable to obtain support for the process of political innovation. This phase can be qualified as successful when the idea is actually selected and obtains support for its subsequent implementation.

Ad 2. Implementing the political innovation

Implementing the political innovation is about taking the required actions to 'make it work'. This involves making budgets available, organizing citizen participation etc. This phase is successful when the political innovation delivers on its political promise. Assessing whether the innovation delivers on its promise is complicated since they embody specific normative choices. At the same time, as we discussed in the previous section, they all aim to result in fair and competent decision-making and therefore these criteria can be used to assess political innovations (Renn and Webler 1995). This means that the performance of political innovations can be assessed in terms of competence and fairness.

Ad 3. Connecting the political innovation to the institutional context

The political innovation needs to be connected to formal and informal arenas of political decision-making and action to have an impact on democratic practice within formal institutions such as parliaments and councils (Goodin and Dryzek 2006). Goodin and Dryzek (2006) actually identify eight forms of impact: actual making policy, taking up in the policy process, informing public debates, shaping policy by market testing, legitimating policy, confidence/constituency building, popular oversight and resisting co-option. We will simplify this distinction in our analysis and we will focus on, on the one hand, actual impact on policies and, on the other, on the legitimation of these policies.

This framework for studying political innovation formed the basis for our empirical research into aleatoric democracy as a political innovation. We conducted empirical research in the City of Utrecht to enhance our understanding of processes of political innovation and, more specifically, the connection of these innovations to political institutions.

Research methods

This study should be regarded as a most advanced case study in terms of the institutional positioning of aleatoric democracy. There have been some experiments with aleatoric democracy but a direct connection with political decision-making by the Municipal Board and the City Council is often not established (Michels 2011, 284). The case we analysed, puts aleatoric democracy right in the heart of political innovation of local democracy and it was nominated for the EUROCITIES Award 2015 in the category 'citizen participation'.

Our empirical study aimed to reconstruct the adoption of a political innovation, the performance of the political innovation and the connection to existing democratic structures. The case was studied intensively from January to November 2015 with a combination of methods:

- Extensive *interviewing* with the responsible Municipal Board Member, interviews with Council Members of each political party responsible for sustainability ($N = 9$), interviews with the experts that informed the citizens about energy ($N = 2$) and interviews with the civil servants that organized the process ($N = 3$).
- A *survey* among the participating citizens during the first and the last meeting ($N = 160$ and 150, response rate = 93 per cent and 90 per cent).
- *Participatory observations* during 4 months of all the meetings of the organizing committee, the three City conversation meetings, a meeting of the Council Committee on public space and a staff meeting between high-ranking civil servants and the Municipal Board Member.
- A wide variety of *documents* was analysed such as memos, draft documents and internal communication at the City of Utrecht, official documents, agendas and minutes of the Council, official communications between Municipal Board Member and Council, and public communications about the energy conversation.

These methods were used to study the phases of the process of political innovation. We studied the *selection of the political innovation* through interviews and by analysing arguments for the aleatoric democracy in documents and meetings. We also interviewed the responsible Municipal Board Member and asked her for the motivations to engage in this process of political innovation. In addition, we asked the Council Members of both coalition and opposition parties for their motivations to engage in or resist to this process of political innovation.

We used the observations of the meeting, the interviews with citizens and the various interviews to analyse the *implementation of the political innovation*. We used a survey among participants to assess the participants' satisfaction with the meetings and the resulting Energy Plan, their reasons for attending and their opinion on the political innovation itself. However, we were not allowed to survey certain background characteristics (such as the level of education) because this could potentially influence the dynamics of the process. Age, gender and area of residence were cross-checked with the municipal registry to assess the representativeness of the group of participants. The political innovation's fairness was assessed by evaluating the extent to which (1) the selection process yielded a representative group of participants, (2) (subsets of) participants could freely take part in the deliberations (and restrictions placed on participation by other participants or members of the organization), (3) participants were allowed to resolve disputes among themselves (i.e. reach a decision) without external arbiters, (4) participants were allowed to influence to the agenda of the meetings (including the predetermined goal of climate neutrality), outcomes of individual meetings and the final Energy Plan. Competence of the political innovation was assessed by evaluating the extent to which (1) participants had access to the required substantive knowledge and expertise to reach an informed decision, (2) this knowledge and expertise was presented in a comprehensive manner, (3) uncertainties surrounding this knowledge and expertise were explicitly relayed to the participants and (4) the process allowed participants to utilize their own knowledge and expertise where possible.

To study the *connection of the political innovation to the institutional context*, we used interviews with the responsible Municipal Board Member and Council Members from both coalition and opposition parties. We focused on the following issues: their overall support for the political innovation, their expectations regarding the capacity of the innovation to legitimize policy, their ideas about the relationship between the democratic positions and mandates of the participants vis-a-vis the Council and their ideas about the motivations of other political actors involved. Process tracing (George and Bennett 2005; Blatter and Haverland 2012) provided theoretical insights in the mechanisms that play a role in the introduction of political innovations in local democracy.

Aleatoric democracy in the City of Utrecht

Political innovation?

In 2014, the newly formed coalition of the Liberal–Democrats, the Greens, the Liberals and the Socialists agreed on an ambitious new target: Utrecht aims to be climate neutral by 2030. In order to craft a realist and well-supported plan, the municipality decided to organize a 'City Conversation on Energy'. The goal of this series of meetings was to allow a 'cross section of the population' to draft a new Energy Plan 2016–2030 (Municipal Board of Utrecht, 10 October 2014). The cross section of the population was to be involved through a random draw selection process, through extensive and informed deliberation and with a financial remuneration.

The process was explicitly aligned with existing political decision-making processes: the Council was to receive its outcomes and the Municipal Board announced its willingness to commit to the adoption of the Energy Plan, provided a fit with the coalition's ambitions. The Municipal Board informed the Council of the conditions for the process, attributing the participants with the task to find out how Utrecht can employ 'all possibilities to save as much energy as possible and generate as much sustainable energy as possible', while confining solutions to the city's own borders (Letter Municipal Board to Council, 28 January 2015).

To understand whether this is a political innovation in the sense of a qualitative change on the basis of a new idea, the new approach can be contrasted with the pre-existing form of political decision-making about urban sustainability. Earlier, wind power development plans for a business park in Utrecht met with fierce local resistance. Invited by the Municipal Board, a local energy cooperative developed an ambitious plan for (eventually) six wind turbines, but after heavy local protest, the Liberal–Democrats and the Social–Democrats in Utrecht withdrew their support in 2013 and the plan lost its majority in the Council (Netherlands Environmental Assessment Agency 2014). In this process, citizens were engaged both as proponents and opponents of the plan. The 'normal' political process engages all citizens through elections but only active citizens, either fighting for sustainable urban living or resisting the location chosen for the windmills, are directly engaged in specific decision-making process.

The new process arguably differs substantially from the traditional process since citizens are engaged through a lottery, rather than through self-selection. Participation came at an early stage in the process, allowing for involvement in the development of plans rather than a mere reaction to already elaborated plans. A participatory, deliberative decision-making model allows for a closer dialogue between stakeholders, not necessarily to arbitrate conflict or to build consensus, but rather to improve understanding of and engagement with each other's positions. This allows to find outcomes that transcend a choice between opposites or a watery consensus, aiming rather to find a model that acknowledges a balance between collective and individual interests. In addition, the remuneration of citizens has the potential of moving beyond 'mere' participation towards governance by the people. A final reason why this is a political innovation is that it changes the interaction between Municipal Board and Council. The Municipal Board Member stipulated beforehand that she would follow the plan developed by the City Conversation on Energy as long as the plan stayed within the framework she had laid out for it (Interview Municipal Board Member, 12 March 2015). This is a highly interesting move since this indicates that she transferred part of her mandate to this group of citizens.

Empirically, the innovativeness of the City Conversation on Energy was contested. The Municipal Board Member and coalition Council Members for the Greens, Liberal–Democrats and Liberals were keen to frame the project as innovative. The City Conversation was referred to as an 'interesting experiment [...] to see how citizens make decisions if they are well-informed' (Interview Municipal Board Member, 12 March 2015). Both Council Members for the Liberal–Democrats and Liberals subscribed to this notion and framed the project as 'an experiment' with the potential to innovate local democracy (Interview D66, 2 April 2015; Interview VVD, 19 March 2015). Other Council Members, including from the fourth coalition party (Socialists), did not emphasize the political or democratic novelty of the City Conversation but regarded it as a normal practice of engaging citizens in conversations on different subjects (Interview CDA, 20 February 2015; Interview CU, 26 March 2015). The Council Member for the Labour Party even called the City Conversations 'make-believe participation' and 'symbolic politics' (Interview PvdA, 12 March 2015).

What is evident from these reactions is that party affiliation appears to be an influential factor in the political assessment of the City Conversation as a political innovation or not. While all parties strongly support the ambition to increase citizen participation in local politics, they disagree about the means to do so. Opposition parties avoid linkages with the project, as they claim the project is bound to fail to produce an Energy Plan that enjoys broad public support. On the other hand, coalition parties tend to support the responsible Municipal Board Member in her claims that a new energy policy for Utrecht requires an innovative experiment to succeed – and that this City Conversation is an important step in that direction. The Socialist Party is the exception to this rule, voicing not only scepticism about the City Conversation as a political innovation but also maintaining political support for the Municipal Board on this project (Interview SP, 5 March 2015).

Selecting the political innovation

A key strategic motivation for the Municipal Board Member to start this process of political innovation was to find a response to citizen resistance to windmills for energy production. The plan to build windmills had received broad support in the City Council but a small group of citizens started a strong protest against these plans and managed to stop the plan. The Municipal Board Member for Sustainability felt that the 'silent majority' had not been heard and that a small group of activist citizens had managed to hijack the debate. For this reason, she wanted to find a way to bring the 'silent majority' into the debate about local energy (Interview Municipal Board Member, 12 March 2015).

The desire to experiment with the idea of aleatoric democracy is another, more idealist, motivation for this political innovation. Aleatoric democracy had received new attention in Flandres in the form of a so-called G1000 and several experiments with this type of democratic arrangement had been organized in the Netherlands. The idea was propagated by the Flemish author David van Reybrouck at a meeting in Utrecht and was received with much appreciation by citizens, public servants, Council Members and the Municipal Board. The idea was seen as a highly interesting political innovation and there was a great willingness to experiment with this idea in Utrecht among public servants, the Municipal Board Member and a limited number of Council Members (Interview Municipal Board Member, 12 March 2015; Interview D66, 2 April 2015; Interview VVD, 19 March 2015). In that sense, the debate about the local energy policy presented an opportunity to experiment with this type of democratic arrangement that was broadly supported by the City Council.

For the Municipal Board Member, the Energy Conversation was an early investment in public and political support for the policy (Interview D66, 2 April 2015). The Municipal Board Member's main concern – stemming from the previous experiences with the windmills – was that everyone supports sustainability measures until they are made visible (Interview Municipal Board Member, 12 March 2015). While the aleatoric element was a novelty, the City Conversation on Energy was the latest addition to a series of City Conversations already taking place in Utrecht. This deliberative method is the showpiece of D66 (Liberal–Democrats), Utrecht's largest party, the Municipal Board Member's strongest coalition partner in environmental affairs and one of two parties that ultimately cancelled the earlier plans for the windmills (Interview GL, 2 March 2015; Interview SP, 5 March 2015). Should the plan draw heavy political fire in the Council, the Municipal Board Member's choice of method would put D66 in a difficult position: withdrawing support for the Energy Plan would mean D66 to discard its own preferred method and the input by citizens it values so strongly.

This analysis shows that an interesting idea popped up and received broad support and was then connected to the strategic interests of the Municipal Board. By involving citizens early in the process and legitimizing the selection of these citizens by using a lottery, the Municipal Board Member hoped to shield herself against opposing citizen initiatives later on in the process by claiming that this was only a 'loud minority' opposing the plan. Similarly, the expectation was also that this would buy her political support and strengthen her position vis-à-vis the Council. The realist positioning of aleatoric democracy as a way to develop a policy plan can be qualified as strategic use of an idealistic perspective on citizen engagement.

Implementing the political innovation

A project team of city civil servants set out to design and organize the City Conversation on Energy. 10,000 citizens received a letter of invitation and 863 sent a positive reply. 200 citizens were then randomly selected in a second stage of the selection process and of these 200 a total of 165 participants attended all three meetings.

The first meeting took place on 14 March 2015 and participants were not yet presented with much technical information but instead were asked to freely imagine what their 'Climate neutral Utrecht' would look like in 2030 (Observations, 14 March 2015). The second meeting was a 'reality check', where the participants' initial ideas were combined with existing policy solutions (Observations, 28 March 2015). In between the second and third meetings the project team and experts created a draft Energy Plan that would serve as input for the final meeting. The aggregation of participants' preferences was predominately done by tallying the preferences. The third and final meeting focused on the evaluation of the draft Energy Plan. Participants were mostly positive about the draft plan: they recognized their input and valued the coherence of the plan. The meeting was concluded with a ceremonial presentation of the Energy Plan to the Municipal Board Member (Observations, 18 April 2015).

The City Conversation on Energy was implemented as means for the Municipal Board Member to gather valuable *political expertise*: insight into the way individual measures are valued by citizens and into the criteria they use to value these measures. In turn, the quality of the obtained political expertise is dependent on two factors: the fairness of the process that allows the entire spectrum of opinions to be taken into account and the competence of the process that ensures the political expertise is informed by a necessary amount technical expertise.

The random selection offered all citizens an equal chance at participation but still only a minority of citizens responded to the invitation. This means that this innovation did not fully comply with the idea of aleatoric democracy but still resulted in a self-selected sample. At the same time, a more diverse group of citizens who were specifically invited participated in the process. For the Municipal Board Member this was of vital importance: the issue of urban energy involves everyone as 'everyone has an outlet' (Interview D66, 2 April 2015). In addition, one of the reasons for offering a remuneration was the argument that all citizens, regardless of economic status, should have an equal chance to participate and, if necessary, the ability to take 3 days off to participate in the City Conversation. The group of participants indeed appeared representative in terms of their age, gender and area of residence, with a slight over-representation of people aged 27–44 (40 per cent of participants, 32 per cent of city population) and 45–64 (29 per cent of participants, 20 per cent of city population). All other percentages fell within a 4-per cent margin of their citywide value (Utrecht Municipal Research Department, 25 February 2015).

The competence of the process was secured by the presence of a number of experts on urban energy (Interview public servant, 12 May 2015; Interview Ecofys, 19 May 2015). Even though there was some doubt about the extent to which the expertise that was brought is was biased by the Municipal Board (Interview VVD, 9 October 2015), these experts provided the participants with the technical expertise necessary to make an informed decision. Emphasis was also placed on the importance of the knowledge and expertise already present among the participants as the chairman notes that everyone is an expert on their own lives and energy use. While early in the process several stakeholders voice concerns over differences in the base levels of knowledge among participants (Interview ChristenUnie, 26 March 2015), the process seems to have created increasingly competent participants (Interview Ecofys, 19 May 2015; Interview public servant, 11 May 2015).

The final verdict on the success of the process lies with the citizens themselves. Our survey shows that 75 per cent believe their ideas have become part of the plan (15.3 per cent is unsure as the plan is not yet adopted by the City Council) and 86 per cent is satisfied with the way the plan has come about. While certain measures were observably more popular than others (e.g. windmills), all participants strongly supported the target of climate neutrality that the plan was supposed to achieve: a majority of participants wanted to remain informal 'energy ambassadors' after the City Conversation on Energy was concluded.

The analysis of this implementation highlights that the idealist logic of realizing a fair and competent form of democracy played a key role in the organization of the aleatoric democracy. Put differently, a fair process was of great strategic importance to the Municipal Board since they could use this as an argument for following the plan drafted by the group of citizens. This shows that the framing of the City Conversation in the earlier phase presents more opportunities for strategic behaviour whereas a process that conforms with certain ideal standards is called for in the implementation of the political innovation.

Connecting the political innovation to the institutional context

From the start, the Municipal Board Member responsible for Sustainability discussed the relation between this form of aleatoric democracy and the existing democratic structures extensively with the City Council. The relation with the City Council was sensitive since the issue here was who spoke on behalf of 'the citizen' and hence there is a certain competition between two democratic mandates – a aleatoric and an electoral – here. The bargaining process between the Municipal Board Member and the Council resulted in specific limits to the mandate for this form of political innovation. The City Conversation on Energy was only to discuss the *means* for realizing climate neutrality in Utrecht by the year 2030. The *ends* for the energy policy were not to be discussed and taken as a given (Interview VVD, 9 November 2015).

The City Conversation on Energy eventually resulted in the Municipal Board's interpretation of the Energy Plan presented to the City Council. The original Energy Plan, as drafted by the citizens, was not forwarded to the Council, but is considered to be the product and property of the 165 participants. The project team also created an additional process report which explains its decisions and the organizational rationale behind the project. The final vote on the plan took place on 14 January 2016 and the plan was unanimously supported by the Council.

The nexus between the City Conversation on Energy as a political innovation and the institutional context can be understood from both an idealist and a realist logic. The two dominant idealist elements are the emphasis on involving the 'silent majority' and offering everyone a chance to participate because the issue of urban energy concerned everyone (Interview Municipal Board Member, 12 March 2015). Such arguments carry much normative weight and are reiterated in the official Municipal Board's interpretation of the Energy Plan (Municipal Board, 2015). The Council has displayed a susceptibility to the normative arguments advanced by the Municipal Board Member. The enhancement of citizen participation was supported by all interviewed Council Members. Moreover, the ambitious target of climate neutrality by 2030 was univocally ratified by the Council prior to the organization of the City Conversation on Energy (Council meeting Commission City & Environment, 12 March 2015). Part of the Council's resistance to the blind adoption of the Energy plan, however, can be ascribed to a normative argument advanced by individual Council Members themselves: the Council still represents the 330,000 citizens that were not invited to the City Conversation (e.g. Interview PvdA, 12 March 2015; Interview SP, 5 March 2015). The absence of clear data on the representativeness of the group of participants kept the conflict between these two idealist arguments (aleatoric vis-a-vis electoral) a central part of the debate between the Council and the Municipal Board Member.

The realist logic in the Council's behaviour highlights a different side of this conflict. The institutionalization of new mechanisms for more direct forms of democracy (such as aleatoric democracy) threaten the relative decrease in power of any elected parliamentary body such as a City Council: if citizens are given a chance to speak directly, they no longer require representation by professional political representatives. The Municipal Board Member explicitly referred to the participants as representatives of the people in the city. Such developments also incentivized

Utrecht's City Council to strategically use its formal powers to block innovation in an attempt to preserve the status quo. The existence of such a strategy is evidenced by the Council's decision not to blindly adopt the Energy Plan as it results from the City Conversation. Of decisive importance for the legitimacy of this decision was the Council's ability to convince other stakeholders of the inability of the participants to come up with the Energy Plan in a fair and competent way. Participants were claimed not to be representative because of their high average level of education (Interview PvdA, 12 March 2015) or their inherent interest in the issue of sustainability: 'You invite 10,000 people for a reason. You only expect 1.5% to show up, and those are the usual suspects" (Interview CDA, 20 February 2015). Moreover, the participants' competence was claimed to be insufficient because energy policy requires an understanding of the technical complexities involved, and this is something 165 participants cannot learn within 3 days (Interview CU, 26 March 2015).

Thus, the executive and legislative powers take opposing sides in the debate on the City Conversation's position in the broader institutional context. However, as the executive power comprised a coalition of Council parties, there is a noticeable difference between the strategies employed by coalition and opposition parties. Coalition parties openly support the Municipal Board Member's decision to organize the City Conversation, but are unwilling to surrender their final say on the resulting Energy Plan. Council Members for the Greens, Liberal–democrats and Liberals attend and enthusiastically participate in one or multiple meetings of the City Conversation. Opposition parties are clearly less supportive of (the Municipal Board Member's decision to use) the method. They are more vocal about the criticisms mentioned above and also emphasize the high-cost-to-low-benefit ratio and the strong possibility of disappointing the participants (Interview ChristenUnie, 26 March 2015; Interview CDA, 20 February 2015). In addition, they purposely stay away from the three meetings because this may implicitly have suggested support for the coalition plans (Interview PvdD, 4 March 2015).

Finally, the participants themselves are well aware of the politicization of the City Conversation. During the final meeting, they clearly state that they do not want to be held accountable for the resulting Energy plan. Moreover, they explicitly refute the Municipal Board Member's claim that the plan is 'Utrecht's plan'. Instead, they suggest that the plan is presented as a plan 'by 166 Utrechters'. (Observations, 18 April 2015)

Based on a realist logic, the construction of the Energy Plan and its preliminary uptake in the Council suggest that the Municipal Board Member's strategy to embed the political innovation into the existing institutional structure has largely been successful. However, a strategic interpretation could read that in this way the Municipal Board Member was able to 'outmanoeuvre' the City Council in an attempt to break the institutional deadlock using citizens to further her own agenda. Complementing this realist logic with its idealist counterpart, a different explanation emerges: the Municipal Board Member was able to break the deadlock to further her own agenda, but this agenda was fully supported by all Council parties. Politicization of the *means* had effectively paralysed a municipal policy area which was striving for a widely supported *goal* and the political innovation broke this deadlock. Moreover, throughout this process, the Municipal Board Member had succeeded in drawing 'normal citizens' closer into the political decision-making process.

Conclusions

The case study shows how the three types of political innovation in Sørensen's (2016) conceptualization – polity, politics and policy – are closely connected in the realization of this form of aleatoric democracy. This innovation is challenging to the existing structure but the analysis clearly shows that aleatoric democracy can indeed find a position in the formal institutionalized democratic system. The old idea was revitalized and resulted in engagement of randomly selected citizens in the development of a plan for a highly sensitive and controversial political issue. Even though there was a self-selection bias since the citizens were not obligated to participate, the case showed new forms of engagement, new roles of citizens and politicians and new outcomes of a political struggle and can therefore be qualified as political innovation. Under what conditions was this political innovations successfully connected to the democratic systems? We have argued that political innovation has two logics: the idealist logic of improving decision-making in the polis and the realist logic of selective use of ideas to realize specific political goals. This case highlights that the intertwinement of these two seemingly competing logics was a key condition for the success of this political innovation.

The idealist logic in the case is that aleatoric democracy indeed has the potential to innovate local politics and contribute to the ability to take decisions about wicked problems such as urban sustainability. The citizens emerged as a new actor on the political stage and their voice was influential. The process of selecting citizens through a lottery resulted in a new type of mandate for the city energy policy. The goal of engaging other citizens than the 'usual suspects' has also been realized and resulted in a varied group of voices. The success of political innovation in this case may be attributed to its early focus on institutional embedding. Acceptance of the value of this form of democracy by both the Municipal Board Member and the City Council were key to its success in terms of impact on urban policies. The aleatoric democracy does not replace the electoral one but strengthens it – although there is also a certain friction – by broadening up citizen engagement by the 'silent majority'.

The realist logic of this process, however, lies in the use of certain ideas in political processes. The idea of the aleatoric democracy is successfully used by the Municipal Board Member and the coalition parties in the Council to build support from 'the citizens' for an Energy Plan. The citizens have been transformed from activists protesting against – but sometimes also in favour of – wind turbines, to a rational advisory body that was able to develop a (much broader) Energy Plan for the city. This Energy Plan was developed within the objectives that had been formulated by the Municipal Board Member and hence could be regarded as an operationalization of her policy agenda. The City Conversation on Energy can be qualified as an instrumental form of political innovation since aleatoric democracy served to break a deadlock in the decision-making process over sustainable energy. The choice for aleatoric democracy, in this logic, is a politically astute move to create legitimacy for the coalition's sustainability agenda.

Our analysis provides some specific insights in the process of political innovation.

First, the empirical analysis of adoption of political innovation shows that we may need to understand this particular case as an example of *garbage can political innovation*. Cohen, March and Olsen (1972) argued that decision-making in organization entails a rather unpredictable coupling between a stream of solutions and a stream of problems. They argue that – metaphorically – problems, solutions, participants and choice opportunities flow in and out of a 'garbage can'. Innovation theory seems to suffer from a similar rationality bias, suggesting that innovation is newly developed solutions to existing problems or possibilities (Rogers 1995). The case study shows that the innovation was not a new but an ancient idea that was connected to a new problem to serve the needs of various, changing participants for different goals. The perspective of garbage can theory – with its attention for windows of opportunities and policy entrepreneurs – can help to understand the 'messy' processes of political innovation.

Second, the analysis highlights the tension between, on the one hand, connecting the innovation to the existing political practices, while on the other hand, also letting it maintain its own democratic profile. The citizens are positioned within a democratic process organized by the Municipal Board Member in contact with the City Council. The ends of collective action were not to be discussed – the goal of reaching climate neutrality in 2030 was a given – and the City Conversation on Energy only focused on the means. Critics argue that this is not in line with the idea of aleatoric democracy where citizens can define their own agenda. At the same time, this embedding of aleatoric democracy in existing democratic institutions may have helped to strengthen the impact of their efforts. The basic tension is that of *compromising political innovation*: more connected political innovations can be expected to be more successful in their embedding but, at the same time, this means that they compromise on their democratic promise.

This research shows how political innovations can be understood from an integrated perspective rather than from a cynical perspective (power always stays in the same hands) or an idealistic perspective (political innovations are free-floating ideas that generate a better world). Our key observation in this case is that the two logics – the idealist and the strategic logic – in political innovation are not rivals but partners. An ideal may only be realized if it is strategically developed and a strategic agenda may only gain legitimacy if it is built on a broadly shared conception of democratic decision-making. Innovative ideas require strategic action and strategic action can benefit from innovative ideas. Our understanding of political innovation needs to take these complementary logics as a starting point for analysis and theory development.

Disclosure statement

No potential conflict of interest was reported by the authors.

References

Barber, B. 1984. *Strong Democracy: Participatory Politics for a New Age*. Berkeley: University of California Press.
Baron, D. 2011. "The Power of the Lot. Are People Obliged to Participate in Political Lotteries?" Unpublished paper presented at ECPR Conference, University of Iceland, Reykjavik, August 27, 2011. http://ecpr.eu/filestore/paperproposal/9fa723db-6eea-4df4-a7cd-63152b4b9c1d.pdf
Bekkers, V., J. Edelenbos, and B. Steijn, eds. 2011. *Innovation in the Public Sector. Linking Capacity and Leadership*. Houndmills: Palgrave MacMillan.
Blatter, J., and M. Haverland. 2012. *Designing Case Studies: Explanatory Approaches in Small-N Research*. Houndmills: Palgrave MacMillan.
Carson, L., and B. Martin. 1999. *Random Selection in Politics*. Westport: Praeger.
Cohen, M. D., J. G. March, and J. P. Olsen. 1972. "A Garbage Can Model of Organizational Choice." *Administrative Science Quarterly* 17 (1): 1–25. doi:10.2307/2392088.
Dahl, R. A. 1998. *On Democracy*. New Haven: Yale University Press.
Dowlen, O. 2008. *The Political Potential of Sortition. A Study of the Random Selection of Citizens for Public Office*. Exeter: Imprint Academic.
Dryzek, J. S. 2000. *Deliberative Democracy and Beyond: Liberals, Critics, Contestations*. Oxford: Oxford University Press.
Effendi, P., and J. Courvisanos. 2012. "Political Aspects of Innovation: Examining Renewable Energy in Australia." *Renewable Energy* 38 (1): 245–252. doi:10.1016/j.renene.2011.07.039.
Fishkin, J. 2009. *When the People Speak: Deliberative Democracy and Public Opinion*. New York: Oxford University Press.
George, A. L., and A. Bennett. 2005. *Case studies and Theory Development in the Social Sciences*. Cambridge, MA: MIT Press.
Goodin, R. E., and J. S. Dryzek. 2006. "Deliberative Impacts: The Macro-Political Uptake of Mini-Publics." *Politics & Society* 34 (2): 219–244. doi:10.1177/0032329206288152.
Hendriks, F., and A. Michels. 2011. "Democracy Transformed? Reforms in Britain and The Netherlands (1990-2010)." *International Journal of Public Administration* 34 (5): 307–317. doi:10.1080/01900692.2011.557815.
Hix, S., and B. Høyland. 2011. *The Political System of the European Union*. 3rd ed. Houndmills: Palgrave MacMillan.
Meijer, A. J. 2014. "From Hero-Innovators to Distributed Heroism: An In-Depth Analysis of the Role of Individuals in Public Sector Innovation." *Public Management Review* 16 (2): 199–216. doi:10.1080/14719037.2013.806575.
Michels, A. 2011. "Innovations in Democratic Governance: How Does Citizen Participation Contribute to a Better Democracy?" *International Review of Administrative Sciences* 77 (2): 275–293. doi:10.1177/0020852311399851.
Morabito, M. S. 2008. "The Adoption of Police Innovation: The Role of the Political Environment." *Policing: An International Journal of Police Strategies & Management* 31 (3): 466–484. doi:10.1108/13639510810895812.
Netherlands Environmental Assessment Agency (PBL). 2014. *Energiecoöperaties: ambities, handelingsperspectief en interactie met gemeenten*. [In Dutch]. Den Haag: Planbureau voor de Leefomgeving.
Osborne, S. P., and L. Brown. 2005. *Managing Change and Innovation in Public Service Organizations*. Milton Park: Routledge.
Pateman, C. 1970. *Participation and Democratic Theory*. Cambridge: Cambridge University Press.
Putnam, R. 2000. *Bowling Alone: The Collapse and Revival of American Community*. New York: Simon & Schuster.
Raghavan, E., and J. Manor. 2012. *Broadening and Deepening Democracy: Political Innovation in Karnataka*. New Delhi: Routledge Books.
Renn, O., and T. Webler. 1995. *Fairness and Competence in Citizen Participation: Evaluating Models for Environmental Discourse*. Vol. 10. Dordrecht: Kluwer Academic Publishers.
Rittel, H., and M. Webber. 1973. "Dilemmas in a General Theory of Planning." *Policy Sciences* 4 (2): 155–169. doi:10.1007/BF01405730.
Rogers, E. M. 1995. *Diffusion of Innovations*. 5th ed. New York: Free Press.

Schudson, M. 1999. *The Good Citizen: A History of American Civic Life.* Cambridge, MA: Harvard University Press.

Smith, G. 2009. *Democratic Innovations: Designing Institutions for Citizen Participation.* Cambridge: Cambridge University Press.

Sørensen, E. 2016. "Political Innovations: Innovations in Political Institutions, Processes and Outputs." *Public Management Review.* doi:10.1080/14719037.2016.1200661

Sørensen, E., and J. Torfing. 2011. "Enhancing Collaborative Innovation in the Public Sector." *Administration & Society* 43 (8): 842–868. doi:10.1177/0095399711418768.

Stone, D. 1997. *Policy Paradox: The Art of Political Decision Making.* New York: W. W. Norton.

van Reybrouck, D. 2013. *Tegen Verkiezingen (Against Elections).* Amsterdam: Bezige Bij.

Walker, J. L. 1969. "The Diffusion of Innovations Among the American States." *American Political Science Review* 63: 880–899. doi:10.2307/1954434.

Webler, T. 1995. "'Right' Discourse in Citizen Participation: An Evaluative Yardstick." In *Fairness and Competence in Citizen Participation: Evaluating Models for Environmental Discourse,* edited by O. Renn, T. Webler, and P. Wiedemann, 35-86. Boston, MA: Kluwer.

Zhang, L. 2012. "The Stages of Political Innovation in Rural China's Local Democratisation: Four Cases of Villagers' Political Innovations." *China Report* 48 (4): 427–448. doi:10.1177/0009445512466620.

Strengthening political leadership and policy innovation through the expansion of collaborative forms of governance

Jacob Torfing and Christopher Ansell

ABSTRACT
This article explores how political leadership and policy innovation can be enhanced through collaborative governance. The main findings are that while wicked and unruly problems create an urgent need for policy innovation, politicians are badly positioned to initiate, drive and lead this innovation. They are either locked into a dependency on policy advice from senior civil servants or locked out of more inclusive policy networks. In either case, they are insulated from fresh ideas and ultimately reduced to 'policy-takers' with limited engagement in policy innovation. Collaborative policy innovation offers a solution to these limitations.

Introduction

This article explores how elected politicians can strengthen both their political leadership and capacity for policy innovation by engaging in processes of multi-actor collaboration that can help them to better understand societal problems and challenges, craft new and creative policy solutions, and generate widespread support for their implementation. Our claim is that by forming and participating in collaborative arenas, politicians can become vehicles for policy innovation, transforming themselves from 'policy-takers' to 'policy-makers'. As such, innovation in policy can be spurred by innovations in politics and the polity (see Sørensen in this issue).

Our point of departure is the urgent need for policy innovation in our increasingly complex and globalized societies in which a growing number of deep-seated and emerging problems appear to be 'wicked and unruly' (Hofstad and Torfing 2016; Ansell and Bartenberger, forthcoming). Problems like climate change, congested cities, integration of refugees, protection of natural resources and social inequalities in health and education are hard to define and even harder to solve due to a complex mixture of cognitive and political constraints. They can neither be solved by standard solutions nor by increasing public spending, but call for innovative out-of-the-box solutions that can break the trade-offs between conflicting goals and externalities that seem to prevent their solution.

Finding innovative policy solutions to wicked and unruly problems presupposes strong political leadership that can help to set the political agenda, frame the problems in new ways, give direction to processes of creative problem-solving, secure widespread support, and commit sufficient resources to the realization of new and bold solutions. Unfortunately, the exercise of political leadership is currently hindered by a number of factors such as globalization, mass mediatization, informatization, anti-authoritarian sentiments and the institutionally embedded idea that politicians should merely focus on overall strategic steering and leave operations to the administration. Politicians generally feel disempowered by global economic pressures, a scandal-focused mass media, information-overload and shortage of knowledge, active citizens who want a direct influence on their living conditions, and the current attempt to reduce their political role to defining overall goals, standards and budget frames and endorsing policy solutions crafted by administrators, experts and advocacy groups. Thus, as wicked and unruly problems proliferate, our political leaders increasingly lack the confidence, opportunity and inputs to initiate and develop innovative solutions.

Both the urgent need for policy innovation and the lack of political leadership can be solved by promoting a more frequent and systematic engagement of politicians in processes of collaborative interaction with public and private actors holding different ideas, competences and resources and by giving politicians a prominent role as sponsors, conveners, facilitators and catalysts of creative problem solving. The point is not that politicians lack formal political power for policy-making, but rather that they are poorly positioned institutionally to contribute to innovative policy solutions. By constructing and participating in collaborative arenas, politicians can place themselves at the centre of policy innovation.

Political leadership is essentially about defining societal problems and challenges, developing new solutions that potentially outperform the existing ones, and mustering political and popular support for their realization (Tucker 1995). Hence, there is an intrinsic relationship between political leadership and policy innovation. Policy innovation depends on the exercise of political leadership, and political leadership is undermined if it fails to develop innovative policy solutions to urgent problems and challenges confronting the political community. Now, since political leaders seldom benefit from divine intervention, their ability to lead by means of defining problems and challenges and designing innovative policy solutions depends on qualified inputs from their surroundings. Politicians cannot create policy innovation in splendid isolation from public and private actors who might hold the keys to understanding a particular problem, fostering a creative and yet feasible solution to it, or facilitating its implementation.

In Western democracies, however, there is a tendency to limit the range of actors who provide input to politicians to a closed circle of executive administrators, policy experts and lobbyists. This tendency is a pity since politicians can benefit tremendously from tapping into the ideas of wider range of relevant and affected actors. More open and systematic collaboration with and between a plethora of public and private actors can enrich politicians' understanding of policy problems, help them to challenge reigning policy paradigms, stimulate creative problem-solving, facilitate a comprehensive assessment of risks and gains of new and bold solutions, provide complementary resources, and help build common ownership that ensures implementation (Hartley, Sørensen, and Torfing 2013). Moreover, politicians who engage in collaborative policy innovation can strengthen their political leadership because their ability to mobilize support from potential followers is enhanced by involving them in the co-creation of new solutions in response to problems that they want to see solved. While the positive impact of multi-actor collaboration on policy innovation and political leadership has always been a possibility, there are two factors currently driving politicians and societal actors towards greater collaborative interaction. First, politicians seem to have an increasing appreciation of the contribution of external actors to policy-making (Christiansen and Nørgaard 2003). Second, the educational and anti-authoritarian revolution from the late 1960s onwards has generated a growing demand among citizens and civil society actors for a more active involvement in policy-making than traditionally offered by representative democracy (Warren 2002). It is unlikely that these two factors alone will be enough to forge a collaborative interface between politicians and relevant policy actors, but they seem to warrant a closer investigation of how collaborative policy-making can enhance policy innovation and strengthen the political leadership of elected politicians.

The present investigation of the collaborative conditions for spurring political leadership and policy innovation is structured in the following way. The constraints on a policy-innovating political leadership are analysed in the second section. The third section defines political leadership, explains the intrinsic link between political leadership and policy innovation and scrutinizes the literature on policy innovation in order to show how politicians seem to be cut off from valuable inputs from external actors. The fourth section explains what politicians might gain from a systematic engagement in collaborative policy innovation and provides examples of what it might look like in practice. The fifth section takes a further look at the drivers and barriers of politicians' engagement in collaborative policy innovation. The conclusion summarizes the findings, discusses when collaborative policy innovation is appropriate and suggests avenues for further research.

Policy innovation and political leadership in Western societies

While the United Nations can report optimistically about major advances in the global war against poverty, disease and illiteracy (United Nations 2015), it is much harder to find examples of successful problem solving through public policy-making in the established Western democracies. Supranational, national, regional and local governments seem to be struggling with a growing number of wicked and unruly problems that are difficult to solve because they are complex, tangled and hard to define, and there is a lack of specialized knowledge about possible solutions, conflicting goals and demands, potential dangers that prevent experimentation, multiple stakeholders with different interests and a high risk of political conflict (Rittel and Webber 1973). Wicked and unruly problems call for innovative solutions, but instead of vigorous efforts to design and implement creative policy solutions, we find an endless parade of political stalemates and logjams. Cases in point include the failure of the European Union to solve the refugee crisis; national governments to reduce CO_2 emissions; regional authorities to stimulate growth and employment in the rural periphery; and local governments to secure social and political inclusion of disadvantaged segments of the population.

Cognitive and political constraints prevent governments from designing innovative policy solutions, but weak political leadership makes things worse and creates a growing popular distrust of elected politicians. The evidence of weak political leadership and bad governance is abundant (Helms 2012). In the United States, Workman, Jones, and Jochim (2009) conclude that Congress not only delegates policy-making authority, but also information-processing to the public bureaucracy, and Meier (2000) claims that the majority of decisions driving public policy in the United States are taken by bureaucrats in the course of policy implementation.

Interestingly, two back-benchers from different sides of the aisle in the Danish parliament recently published a critical analysis of how their political leadership role is reduced to voting for or against bills drafted by executive civil servants and expert committees with limited involvement of members of parliament (MPs) (Bruus and Lauritzen 2014, 2015). Their analysis sparked lively discussions in the Danish parliament about the conditions for political leadership of elected politicians and proposals for reforms of the parliamentary system of standing committees (Folketinget 2015). Equally interesting, a Danish municipality recently discovered that the local councillors in 2014 had followed the recommendations of the executive civil servants in 98.6 per cent of all the political decisions taken by the local council (Sørensen and Torfing 2015). This discovery adds flesh and blood to the results of a recent survey showing that 66 per cent of local councillors in Denmark believed that the biggest problem they face is their lack of influence on the political development of the municipality (DJØF 2013). These reports are by no means exceptional.

Several factors can help us to explain the elected politicians' perception of the constraints on their political leadership. First, globalization of economic transactions, physical and virtual communication and the strategic horizons of public governance mean that political jurisdictions at the local, regional and national level are subjected to pressures from processes that they can neither control nor affect because power is horizontally and vertically dispersed and the institutional mechanisms for integrative political leadership are weak. To make matters worse, many politicians seem to subscribe to the idea that the external pressures emanating from economic globalization dictate a particular type of neoliberal economic policies. Hence, the frequent use of the political catchphrase stating that: 'There is no alternative'. The global market economy is perceived as a self-governing mechanism that leaves elected politicians as mere bystanders.

Second, the ongoing mediatization of society and politics has created a drama democracy that places a high premium on personal point scoring, political conflict and rivalry, populist rhetoric and short-term solutions that hardly match the problems at hand. The result is the decline of informed political debate, trust-based political collaboration, shared focus on salient political issues and the production of long-term solutions addressing wicked and unruly problems (Klijn 2014).

Third, technologically enabled informatization means that there is unlimited access to multiple, redundant, parallel and competing streams of information that create a paralyzing information overload while, at the same time, a scarcity of validated and reliable knowledge that politicians can act upon (Workman, Jones, and Jochim 2009). Time constraints force politicians to delegate information processing to public administrators who become much more knowledgeable and powerful than the politicians they are serving.

Fourth, anti-authoritarian sentiments nurtured by rising competences and political empowerment mean that citizens have less faith in expert knowledge and political elites and increasing confidence in their own ability to participate in and be able to influence public decision making (Warren 2002). Hence, elected politicians are under pressure to engage with citizens who are no longer satisfied with their role as passive spectators, but demand to be actively involved in decisions affecting their lives (Bang and Sørensen 1999).

Last but not least, the New Public Management suggests that elected politicians should perceive themselves as members of a corporate board. Hence, they should stand at the bridge of the ship and do the overall strategic steering once every year and otherwise be tied to the mast and keep their fingers off the daily operations of public service organizations. Although the emphasis on strategic steering aims to save politicians from drowning in administrative details, many politicians become utterly frustrated because they lack the strategic competences required to define overall goals, standards and budget frames and because the corporatization of their political role cuts them off from the real-life policy problems that motivated them to pursue a political carrier in the first place (Christensen and Lægreid 2001).

Studies of political leadership and policy innovation

At the generic level, leadership can be defined as the attempt of one or more persons to influence the behaviour of a group of actors in order to realize a particular set of goals (Parry and Bryman 2006). When we speak of political leadership, the goals pursued through the exercise of leadership are limited neither to the profit motives of a private firm nor to the organizational objectives of a voluntary organization, but are political goals for society at large. In liberal democracies the political goals are defined by the people in and through regular elections and public deliberations.

Political leadership clearly involves the exercise of power in terms of the ability to make authoritative decisions that mobilize public resources in the pursuit of a public purpose. However, we should be careful not to reduce political power to domination and force. Although political leaders may have many forms of 'hard power' at their disposal, they frequently make use of 'soft power' that 'co-opts people rather than coerces them' and 'rests on the ability to shape the preferences of others to want what you want' (Nye 2010, 307; Helms 2012, 6). Political leadership is exercised in and through a mutual relationship between political leaders and a more or less active and outspoken group of followers. The political leaders play a crucial role in constructing the political community that they are leading, but their followers critically evaluate the political leaders and may challenge them or shift their allegiance if they are dissatisfied.

According to Tucker (1995), political leadership undertakes three crucial functions: (1) providing a diagnosis of the societal problems and challenges that need to be addressed; (2) proposing a set of visionary, yet feasible, solutions to the problems and challenges at hand; and (3) generating support and mobilizing resources for the realization of the proposed solutions. As such, political leadership is essentially transformative as it involves higher order changes in needs, values, beliefs and practices (Burns 2003). In stable societies with only a limited number of relatively small problems, it is sufficient for transformative political leaders to marginally adjust existing policies and strategies. In times of crisis and increasing turbulence, where demographic, socioeconomic and environmental changes threaten the welfare and security of the population and where wicked and unruly problems proliferate, political leaders must necessarily engage in policy innovation.

Policy innovation is a particular type of innovation that aims to respond to wicked and unruly public problems or to realize ambitious new political agendas by (1) redefining policy problems and opportunities; (2) reformulating basic goals and priorities; (3) developing new problem-solving strategies; and (4) deploying new policy tools and perhaps even creating new governance structures. Although policy innovation does not necessarily advance all of these changes to the same degree, the combined effect of these changes should produce a rupture with established practice and common wisdom in a particular policy context. In short, policy innovation requires what Peter Hall calls second- or third-order policy change and thus a high degree of reflexivity. Since policy innovation is likely to disrupt distributional outcomes as well as the roles, identities and habitual practices of social and political actors, it is likely to generate considerable resistance that must be overcome through the exercise of skilful political leadership combining soft and hard power.

The scholarly focus on political leaders' contribution to policy innovation is by no means new. In his 1984 book *Political Innovation in America*, Polsby analyses the role of politicians in fostering policy innovation. According to Polsby, politicians are driven by the competition for voters and will exploit ritualized occasions such as election campaigns, press briefings, party conferences and presidential addresses to the nation to market new and innovative policy solutions that can win support from the electorate. However, while politicians might play a key role in identifying and legitimizing the problems and unfulfilled needs that call for policy innovation and in assessing the political distributional consequences of new policies, they seem to play a limited role in framing policy problems, developing the substance of new policy proposals and evaluating their likely effects and outcomes (Polsby 1984, 55). The definition of problems and the development and evaluation of new policy solutions is more often than not left to executive civil servants and their aids with occasional assistance from scientific experts. Sometimes politicians are not even involved in identifying the pressing problems and needs, but are merely searching for something to offer the electorate. As Polsby concludes: 'one process invents an alternative, nurtures it, floats it into the subculture of decision-makers; another process searches for ideas, finds them, renovates them for immediate use, and exploits them politically' (Polsby 1984). If this is so, it means that policy-making takes the form of a 'garbage can process' where solutions precede the problems (Cohen, March, and Olsen 1972). It also means that politicians play a limited role in policy innovation and rely heavily on their administrative staff. As such, political leadership is reduced to picking the right policy to offer the electorate at some mediatized event, and policy innovation suffers from the heavy reliance on bureaucratic views and ideas, spiced up with expert opinions and adjusted in accordance with the anticipation of what leading politicians will find politically appropriate.

Kingdon (1984) agrees with the basic line of argument set out by Polsby. He also conceives policy innovation as a process through which policy entrepreneurs contingently connect separate streams of problems, solutions and political opinions, and he believes that there are certain patterns in how this is done. However, on the basis of empirical studies of the US Congress, he seems to put more emphasis on the interaction between appointed political officials, executive civil servants and members of the elected assemblies, and to the actors inside government he adds the actors outside government including interest groups, academics, researchers, consultants and mass media. In the United States the president and the executive office play a key role in setting the agenda, but Congress is highly effective in offering alternatives from which to choose during the policy process. The presidential staff and the politically appointed officials in departments and bureaus both play a crucial role in agenda setting and the generation of policy alternatives, while career bureaucrats seem to play a less prominent role. Actors outside government also have considerable influence on policy innovation. The less visibility a policy issue has and the less ideological and partisan the debate about it is, the more influence interest groups will tend to have. Academics, researchers and consultants may also influence the policy process and contribute to policy innovation, but their influence varies across policy areas. Mass media, however, seems to have less influence than is commonly assumed. Hence, according to Kingdon, elected politicians do not dominate the policy process in the way that they are expected to in liberal democracies, but the same goes for the other actors. Nobody is really in charge. Elected politicians and their executive civil servants are very important for fostering policy innovation, but only when they are supported by other actors. This observation seems to introduce a coalition perspective. Consensus-based policy coalitions that link problems, solutions and political opinions in contingent ways may be formed through bargaining processes that eventually lead to policy innovation. In sum, while Polsby imagined politicians cherry-picking new policy ideas from the public bureaucracy, Kingdon sees politicians as a part of a broader change coalition involving non-governmental actors.

The focus on policy coalitions is further expanded in the literature on policy networks that emphasizes the resource dependencies and/or shared belief systems that unify public and private actors engaged in sector-specific policy making (Kenis and Schneider 1991; Marsh and Rhodes 1992). The policy network literature has a keen eye for the broad range of actors engaged in the design and/or implementation of public policy, but it also reveals two important problems. First, elected politicians seem to play a marginal role in policy networks. They are seldom present in the councils, committees and meetings in which public managers and representatives of different interest groups negotiate and shape public policies, and when they try to play a role in policy networks they often end up relying heavily on the public managers who are managing the networks (Koppenjan, Kars, and Voort 2009). Second, the policy network literature tends to treat networks as instruments for pursuing particular organizational or sector-specific interests rather than acting as vehicles of policy innovation. At least, highly influential and tightly knit policy communities seem to be less innovative than the not so influential and more loosely structured issue networks when it comes to policy-making (Marsh and Rhodes 1992). This insight is echoed by researchers from advocacy coalition theory who find that narrow coalitions based on normative core beliefs may not be broad-based enough to facilitate policy innovation (Ansell, Reckhow, and Kelly 2009). So the paradox is that while the policy network literature expands the range of actors engaged in policy-making and further distributes political power between them, it diminishes the role of politicians by displacing the centre of gravity of policy-making beyond the easy access of politicians and allows policy arenas to be captured by a logic of interest protection rather than a logic of policy innovation.

Nevertheless, a more innovation-friendly interpretation of policy networks is offered by Sabatier and Jenkins-Smith (1993), who emphasize the role of policy learning in fostering policy innovation. Policy learning, defined as changes in the distribution of beliefs in a network, is induced by individual attitude change, diffusion of new beliefs, turnover of network participants, group conflicts and communicative responses to external events. Policy learning changes the understanding of the relative status of particular goals and values and the causal assumptions about which policy tools and institutional frameworks can help to realize these goals and values in practice. Learning that problematizes core assumptions about goals, values and causal mechanisms while simultaneously, aiming to respond to new external events and incorporating new insights generated elsewhere is a prerequisite for policy innovation. There are also good reasons to believe that learning is accelerated by multi-actor collaboration that allows different public and private actors to draw on different sources of knowledge when challenging and criticizing each other's beliefs and assumptions and subsequently trying to integrate these into more or less coherent policies. In short, collaboration tends to facilitate expansive and transformative learning, which in turn tends to spur policy innovation (Mezirow 2000; Engeström 2008; Torfing 2016).

This insight has important consequences since it urges politicians to engage more frequently and systematically in a collaborative exchange of experience, knowledge, ideas etc. with other public and private actors. Politicians must get out of parliamentary committees and City Hall and interact with the relevant and affected actors who can help them to understand the complex character of the problem at hand, to develop and test new policy solutions, and adjust them so that they work in practice and produce the desired results. When successful, collaborative policy innovation can help elected politicians to strengthen their political leadership by creating broad ownership for a new set of political goals, problem definitions and policy tools.

Examples of politicians engaged in collaborative policy innovation

Despite the obvious advantages of a more collaborative leadership style, it is an open question whether it will be possible to engage busy, media-focused politicians in deliberative processes aiming to foster innovative policies. Many politicians will tend to consider themselves as sovereign decision-makers who, as elected representatives of the people, have all the power and all the political responsibility, which they are not supposed to share with non-elected actors. While recognizing this and other impediments to collaborative policy innovation, we would like to draw attention to some interesting new examples of what collaborative policy innovation might look like in practice. These illustrative examples may not describe the typical ways that politicians engage in the development of new policies. Indeed some of the examples are relatively ground-breaking. Still, the examples attest to the feasibility of collaborative policy innovation, and learning from them may help us to do more of it in the future.

To demonstrate the prevalence and empirical variability of collaborative policy innovation, we have selected an example from the local, regional and national levels. Our descriptive analysis focuses on: (1) how collaborative forums and arenas are created and sustained; (2) how innovative policy solutions are initiated, crafted and agreed upon; and (3) how politicians can lead and manage collaborative policy innovation. While the first question concerns the institutional design of collaborative policy innovation, the second concerns the processes through which differences are constructively managed in the pursuit of innovation, and the third focuses on the political legitimacy and democratic anchorage of collaborative policy innovation.

Local Task Committees in Gentofte Municipality, Denmark

Gentofte Municipality had experimented with participatory and collaborative policy innovation for several years when it decided in 2015 to reorganize the way that the local councillors work as politicians (Sørensen and Torfing 2015). The goal of the organizational reform is to enhance the opportunities for the local councillors to focus on policy development and do it together with citizens and local stakeholders. In order to facilitate this process, the City Council has created eight so-called Task Committees that are temporary, advisory and thematic committees composed of a select group of local councillors, relevant and affected citizens, and local stakeholder organizations who will together engage in the development of innovative solutions to the most pressing local policy problems. The City Council defines the remit and appoints the members of the Task Committees (typically five politicians and ten citizens/stakeholders), but the members can make their own plans for meetings and activities and also decide to involve additional citizens and stakeholders through sub-committees, task forces, social media, public hearings etc. Since in Denmark all the local councillors (except the mayor) are doing unpaid voluntary work for the City Council, often while holding a regular job, their time budget is restricted. Hence, in order to find time and space for the politicians to work in the new Task Committees, it has been decided that the activities of the standing political committees will be scaled down, so that instead of eleven meetings per year, they will only have four short two-hour meetings. Moreover, instead of closely monitoring the daily operations of the administration, the new standing committees should focus on overall policy performance. If the standing committees identify problems and challenges that call for political action, they can either craft a new set of guidelines for the administration or suggest the creation of a new Task Committee and begin to draft a remit for it. In the Task Committee the politicians combine overall strategic goals with concrete experiences and ideas from the other participants and input from the administrators who service the Task Committee and facilitate its meetings. The Task Committees meet on a regular basis over a flexible period from 3 to 18 months in order to gather information, define and frame the problem, search for innovative solutions, and discuss their practical and political feasibility. In the end a report is sent to the political committee responsible for the particular policy area, which makes policy recommendations to the City Council on the basis of the report. The elected politicians exercise political leadership by initiating and participating in the Task Committees, which in the Danish context provide ground-breaking forums for collaborative policy innovation. The politicians are also deciding whether to adopt the collaborative policy recommendations. However, their political leadership is transformed since they are leading processes of collaborative innovation in which they have to convene, interact with and take account of the opinions, ideas and proposals of local citizens and stakeholders. Their political leadership is neither reduced to offering symbolic solutions to the electorate nor simply ratify administrative proposal, but now involves co-initiation, co-design and co-implementation of innovative policy solutions.

Regional innovation networks in Venlo, the Netherlands

The Venlo region in the southeast part of the Netherlands used to be a thriving agricultural area supported by agricultural research institutions and an excellent infrastructure connecting it to Germany. However, at the turn of the millennium it suffered from economic decline and environmental problems that led many young people to leave the region (Termeer and Nooteboom 2014). In the Netherlands such problems used to be tackled by corporatist arrangements, but the failure of these arrangements to deal with the negative externalities of agricultural modernization undermined their power and paved the way for the construction of a new green growth alliance. Business leaders from the Venlo region met to discuss their common concerns for the future development of the region and the urgent need for action. After a while they managed to involve regional politicians in their ambitious plan to develop an innovative strategy for green growth. An informal regional network of business people, elected politicians and civil servants was formed and soon managed to get support from local municipalities and government officials. The informal network enabled and supported the formation of the Foundation for Regional Dialogue that was a broader and more formal network driving the development of the Venlo Greenport Project. The new formal network was led by a core group that comprised members appointed by all the participating organizations from the public, for-profit and non-profit sectors. The core group organized a series of meetings and workshops that led to the formulation of an innovative regional development strategy aiming to enhance sustainable farming and it also facilitated and sponsored the crafting and testing of innovative projects. As the number of project proposals increased and the need for evaluating and monitoring these projects grew, the core group was replaced with a more formal Network Board consisting of formal leaders from government, business, education and research. The collaborative innovation process created a continuous spin-off in terms of small informal change alliances that developed ideas and projects later adopted by the formal network. Elected politicians did not play a privileged role in the collaborative innovation process. Hence, the exercise of adaptive and enabling leadership was distributed among a plethora of public and private actors. Nevertheless, elected politicians and their civil servants played an important role in terms of providing funding and legitimacy to the Venlo Greenport project.

Statewide citizens' juries on energy policy in New South Wales, Australia

While politicians usually have few problems generating public interest in energy-related topics such as climate change and local infrastructure projects, it is more difficult to solicit input to policy innovation in the more mundane field concerning the production and distribution of energy. In the State of New South Wales (NSW) in Australia, politicians have sought to change that by supplementing the standard policy consultation procedures based on public hearings and written submission from key stakeholders with the formation of citizen juries (Hendriks 2013). The collaborative policy process was orchestrated by MPs from the Public Accounts Committee (PAC) who recruited fifty-four randomly selected citizens from an urban centre (Sydney) and a rural area (Tamworth) to serve on two concurrent citizens' juries. These deliberative bodies were asked to consider the barriers to and to recommend a course of action with regard to alternative forms of energy generation. Both juries met 4–5 times over a period of ten weeks in the summer of 2012 before submitting a report to the PAC that fed into the preparation of its own report to parliament, which was published in late 2012 (PAC 2012). The recommendations from the citizens' reports were summarized in a separate chapter in the official PAC report and the reports were included in the appendices. Studies show that the citizens' reports had a real impact on the MP's recommendations to the NSW parliament, although some of the more controversial proposals were either not addressed or addressed and rejected (Hendriks 2013). The MPs in the PAC played an active role in setting up and briefing the two citizens' juries and also processed their recommendations. The MPs also met personally with the citizens when they attended meetings in the citizens' juries.

Table 1 provides a comparison of the three cases of collaborative policy innovation, revealing a number of differences and similarities in terms of the institutional arenas for policy interaction, the process of collaborative innovation and the leadership role of the politicians.

As indicated in Table 1, the Task Committees and the citizens' juries differ from the regional innovation networks by being formal and politically initiated. At the same time, they differ from each other since the Task Committees are permanent institutions integrated into the legislative structures while the citizens' juries are temporary and supplementary. In contrast to the citizens' juries, where the politicians receive recommendations based on citizens' deliberations, both the Task Committees and the regional innovation networks facilitate joint deliberation between politicians and external actors. The main difference between the Task Committees and the regional innovation networks is that the latter fail to involve ordinary citizens. Political leadership of the process of collaborative policy innovation is stronger in the Task Committees and citizens' juries than in the regional innovation networks, but it is only in the Task Committees that the politicians gets to interact with citizen deliberators.

Table 1. Comparison of the cases of collaborative policy innovation.

	Institutional arena of interaction	Collaborative innovation process	Leadership role of politicians
Local task committees	Permanent and formal arena formed by legislative body and integrated into the existing legislative structures	Joint deliberation between politicians, citizens, stakeholders and civil servants	Politicians orchestrate, participate in and assess outcomes of the collaborative innovation process
Regional innovation networks	Private actors form a temporary, informal network arena that spurs the formation of a broader and more formal network of public and private actors	Joint deliberation between politicians, stakeholders and civil servants	Politicians play a limited role as champions and sponsors of collaborative innovation as political leadership is dispersed in relatively informal networks
Statewide citizens' juries	Temporary, but formal arena formed by legislative body supplementing existing legislative structures	No joint deliberation as recommendations based on citizens' deliberations are relayed to politicians	Politicians orchestrate and assess outcomes of the collaborative innovation process

In sum, although our analysis does not allow us to draw any inference about the causal relationship between the institutional design, process and leadership of multi-actor collaboration and the resulting policy innovations, the Task Committees seem to have some comparative advantages in terms of being permanent and highly transparent institutional designs that facilitate joint deliberation between politicians and relevant external actors through a well-structured process where political leaders are allowed to play a decisive role.

Drivers and barriers of collaborative policy innovation

As partly illustrated by the empirical examples above, politicians' participation in and leadership of more or less institutionalized processes of collaborative policy innovation may help them to break policy deadlocks, connect and communicate with different groups of experts, stakeholders and citizens, and discursively construct the political community that they aim to lead. The potential gains raise the question of what drives and hinders a more frequent and systematic engagement of politicians in collaborative policy innovation.

One of the drivers that may urge politicians to go further down this road is the alarming decline in citizens' trust in politicians, which is a thorn in the side of elected politicians because both their personal political legitimacy and the democratic legitimacy of the entire system of government depend on a high level of popular trust. In the final instance the lack of trust reduces the ability of elected politicians to implement structural reforms and secure compliance with public regulation (OECD 2013). As such, political officials increasingly recognize, especially within the European Union (European Commission 2001a, 2001b, 2003, 2005), that the level of political trust needs to be improved and that this requires increased collaboration with citizens and private stakeholders in order to develop and implement innovative solutions that enhance public performance and satisfy unfulfilled social needs (Skelcher and Torfing 2010).

Another driver is elected politicians' dissatisfaction with being sidelined and marginalized by technocratic policy-making spearheaded by policy experts and executive civil servants. Politicians who are part of government or hold important positions in political committees surely have better chances to match the strong influence of experts and senior administrators than backbenchers, but even ministers can be sidelined by the administrative mandarins (Christensen 1983; Hood and Lodge 2006). Even well-positioned politicians will, therefore, be likely to welcome collaboration with actors outside government that can inspire them to pursue new and innovative ideas that administrators would deem 'inappropriate' from a strictly administrative point of view.

A third driver is the suppressed eagerness of elected politicians to solve societal problems and challenges, which is often what originally motivated them to go into politics. Many politicians are frustrated by the role prescription of New Public Management, which basically tells them to act as a board of directors that defines the overall goals and strategies and monitors performance. They may therefore be inclined to find new ways of legitimately engaging in problem-solving together with societal actors who like themselves are driven by values, indignation and other forms of political passion and who can help them to better understand the problems at hand and to design, test and realize innovative solutions (Sørensen 2006).

A last driver is the frustration that many politicians feel when they are forced to defend new policy solutions against criticisms from citizens and relevant stakeholders in the mass media, or in public hearings and debates. When new policy proposals resting on carefully calibrated political compromises and followed up by elaborate administrative plans for their implementation, politicians are often prevented from making political concessions, even if they want to, and that is a persistent source of frustration. An obvious solution to this problem would be to involve citizens and stakeholders in collaborative processes that allows them to influence the initiation, design and perhaps even the implementation of policy innovations. Co-creation of new policy solutions will allow adaptation of new policy proposals to the needs and demands of citizens and relevant stakeholders and that will build a joint ownership for the new solutions.

Before getting carried away by the potential drivers of collaborative policy innovation, let us take a close and sobering look at the barriers that must be overcome in order to engage politicians in collaborative processes. We have already mentioned one fundamental barrier in terms of the classical democratic self-perception of politicians as the 'elected representatives of the people' who are expected to use their skills and power to govern and provide solutions for the people rather than involving the electorate in complex decision-making processes that ordinary people can neither be expected to understand nor take responsibility for. The negative effect of this role perception on collaborative engagement is exacerbated by the New Public Management idea that politicians should focus on 'steering' the ship, and leave the 'rowing' to professional administrators (Osborne and Gaebler 1993). The result of this reassertion of the politics–administration divide is that politicians become insulated from the forums and networks through which public governance is produced and delivered and problems are identified and solved.

Another barrier is that politicians who are driven by ideology, and perhaps even strive for ideological purity – as we have seen recently with the American Tea Party movement – will find it difficult to engage in an open-minded debate with citizens and stakeholders that aspires to find innovative, yet feasible, solutions to urgent problems and challenges. Dogmatic and uncompromising ideological sentiments and pragmatic problem-solving do not go well together (Ansell 2011).

A third barrier is the competition within and between political parties. Representative democracy is built on this competition for votes, media attention, and political control, making it a challenge to openly share ideas and engage in cooperative enterprise. This barrier is somewhat less accentuated in consensual democracies as opposed to majoritarian winner-take-all democracies (Lijphart 2012). However, even in more consensual democracies, adversarial interaction can dominate, reducing opportunities for collaborative policy innovation.

A fourth barrier is the unwillingness of politicians to accept the risks associated with policy innovation, particularly in the pre-election phase. In our mediatized drama democracy, the penalty for policy failure is large and may wreck political careers, especially if politicians have invested personal prestige and integrity in the design of the new policy. Although collaborative policy innovation offers a way of sharing the responsibility for both success and failure with other actors, the danger of being left alone with the responsibility for policies that do not work as expected or create unforeseen negative externalities may discourage politicians from participating in collaborative policy innovation.

Last but not least, we would like to mention about the scarcity of time and resources that politicians have at their disposal either due to their status as unpaid political volunteers holding a full-time job while serving as local or regional councillors, or due to the large amount of time spent on fundraising for the next election campaign, which is a well-known problem at state or federal level government in the United States. Collaborative policy-making takes lots of time and this time must be found by reforming the institutions of representative democracy. Public financing of political parties and reform of the standing committee system may offer a way forward.

The barriers for politicians to engage in multi-actor collaboration and pursue policy innovation are considerable. Although it is also possible to identify strong drivers, researchers and practitioners will have to work hard to overcome the barriers by developing institutional designs and role perceptions that enable elected politicians to embrace the expansion of processes of collaborative policy innovation.

Concluding remarks

We have aimed to explore how political leadership and policy innovation can be enhanced through *polity innovations* that create new platforms for collaborative governance in which politicians play a central role and *innovations in politics* that foster processes of collaborative innovation in which differences are constructively managed in the pursuit of innovation. The main finding is that wicked and unruly problems create an urgent need for policy innovation, but that politicians are badly positioned to initiate, drive and lead policy innovation. They are either locked into a dependency on policy advice from senior civil servants or locked out of more inclusive but sealed off policy networks. In either case, politicians are insulated from fresh ideas and are ultimately reduced to policy-takers with a limited role in policy innovation. Collaborative policy innovation is a solution to these limitations insofar as the creation of institutional arenas facilitates the participation of a wide set of public and private actors who can perturb existing assumptions and paradigms and contribute to new change theories. The institutional design of collaborative arenas should also ensure that politicians have a clear presence and a leadership role that can prevent the arena from being co-opted for the narrow protection of interests. Finally the design should facilitate deliberation and policy learning among the participating actors.

Our argument is premised on the observation that political leaders need to spur policy innovation in order to find new and better ways of dealing with wicked and unruly problems and that policy innovation can help them mobilize active support from their followers and widen their appeal. However, we should bear in mind that policy innovation in itself is neither good nor bad (Hartley 2005). Although innovation processes tend to be driven by the intention to improve the public sector by enhancing its problem-solving capacity, increasing the quality of public services and reducing costs, the results of policy innovation might not be as expected and might not be liked by everybody. Moreover, there are some areas where policy innovation should be pursued with caution because the risks are considerable (e.g. innovative pension reforms may cause a future income loss for particular groups of citizens) and policy failure can be fatal (e.g. policies for safety regulation of nuclear power plants or air traffic). As such, it is an integral part of political leadership to determine whether or not to initiate policy innovation in a particular policy field.

We have recommended a collaborative approach to policy innovation because collaboration seems to spur the development of innovative solutions. Collaborative policy innovation will in turn help to strengthen political leadership in the age of governance in which no public or private actor seems to possess all the knowledge and resources necessary to steer society and the economy (Kooiman 1993). However, collaborative policy innovation may not be feasible to the same degree at all times, in all areas, at all levels of government and in all political systems. In acute crisis situations where new policies must be developed over night, there might not be time for lengthy collaborative processes. In policy areas dealing with highly technical or confidential issues pertaining to environmental regulation, public security or private business opportunities a collaborative approach may not be an obvious choice. At the federal and national level it will sometimes be difficult to find ways of involving citizens, whereas at regional and local levels of government there is a greater proximity to citizens who can engage in collaborative policy-making. Finally, political systems with a tradition of corporatist involvement of stakeholders or with distributed powers nurturing bipartisan negotiation may on the whole be more conducive to collaborative policy innovation than political systems based on sovereign decision-making by the political and administrative centre of a unitary state or winner-take-all political contests.

In this article we have merely tried to set an agenda for further research, and we are perfectly aware that there is a long way to go before we fully understand how politicians can gain from collaborative policy innovation and under what circumstances. The next steps will have to include a more systematic mapping of examples of how politicians engage in collaborative policy innovation and comparative analysis of the political and institutional factors conditioning success and failure. As such, an initial expansion of exploratory in-depth case studies must be supplemented with more rigorous comparisons across cases, leading to the development and testing of hypotheses that aim to explain the dynamics of collaborative policy innovation and the results they produce, both in terms of new and better policy solutions and in terms of a stronger political leadership.

Empirical studies must be supported by theory development and a central point is here to re-conceptualize political leadership in order to discover what it can mean in the context of collaborative governance (Ansell and Gash 2008). As pointed out by Helms (2012, 2-3), there is an unresolved tension between the concept of political leadership and the basic thrust of collaborative governance. Although political leadership is not necessarily linked to the exercise of hard power in formal, hierarchical organizations, it is clearly associated with the creation of followership, while governance tends to blur the distinction between leaders and followers. Moreover, whereas political leadership is often thought of in terms of individual action, the governance paradigm stresses relations of interdependency between public and private actors. Finally, while political leadership is conceptually tied to the exercise of power, there seems to be little focus on power in the literature on governance (see Torfing et al. 2012). These fundamental differences call for theoretical discussions and clarifications that can inform and guide empirical studies.

The potential impact of research and experiments with collaborative policy innovation is huge as it may affect the ability of politicians worldwide to strengthen their political leadership in and through pragmatic and creative problem-solving. However, in order to fully grasp the conditions for and mechanisms of collaborative policy innovation we need to bring together groups of researchers that do not normally work together. Hence, researchers in the field of public governance and public innovation research must join forces with researchers with scholarly expertise in political parties and executives. Institutional separations and cultural differences may prevent such a marriage, but as cross-disciplinary research becomes more and more fashionable there is a hope that these different groups of academics can develop a fruitful and mutually beneficial cooperation.

Disclosure statement

No potential conflict of interest was reported by the authors.

References

Ansell, C. 2011. *Pragmatist Democracy: Evolutionary Learning as Public Philosophy.* Oxford: Oxford University Press.
Ansell, C., and M. Bartenberger. Forthcoming. "Unruly Problems." In *Governance in Turbulence Times*, edited by C. Ansell, J. Trondal, and M. Øgård. Oxford: Oxford University Press.
Ansell, C., and A. Gash. 2008. "Collaborative Governance in Theory and Practice." *Journal of Public Administration Research and Theory* 18 (4): 543–571.
Ansell, C., A. Reckhow, and A. Kelly. 2009. "'How to Reform a Reform Coalitions: Outreach, Agenda Expansion, and Brokerage in Urban School Reform'." *Policy Studies Journal* 37 (4): 717–743. doi:10.1111/j.1541-0072.2009.00332.x.
Bang, H. P., and E. Sørensen 1999. "The Everyday Maker: A New Challenge to Democratic Governance." *Administrative Theory & Praxis* 21 (3): 325–341.
Bruus, J., and K. Lauritzen 2014. "Folkestyre Eller Ekspertvælde." Berlingske Tidende, April 18.
Bruus, J., and K. Lauritzen 2015., "Regeringens Magt – Folketingets Afmagt." Berlingske Tidende, February 13.
Burns, J. M. 2003. *Transforming Leadership.* New York, NY: Grove Press.
Christensen, J. G. 1983. "Mandariner og Minister." *Politica* 15 (3): 284–304.
Christiansen, P. M., and A. S. Nørgaard. 2003. *Faste forhold, flygtige forbindelse.* Aarhus: Aarhus University Press.
Christensen, T., and P. Lægreid. 2001. *NPM – The Transformation of Ideas and Practice.* Aldershot: Ashgate.
Cohen, M., J. G. March, and J. P. Olsen. 1972. "A Garbage Can Model of Organizational Choice." *Administrative Science Quarterly* 17 (1): 1–25. doi:10.2307/2392088.
DJØF. 2013. *Faktaark om kommunalpolitikernes arbejde.* Copenhagen: DJØF.
Engeström, Y. 2008. *From Teams to Knots: Activity-Theoretical Studies of Collaboration and Learning at Work.* New York, NY: Cambridge University Press.
European Commission 2001a, "European Governance: A White Paper." COM(2001) 428 final, Brussels: European Commission.
European Commission. 2001b. *Networking People for Good Governance in Europe.* Brussels: European Commission.
European Commission 2003. *The Interactive Policy-making Initiative.* http://ec.europa.eu/yourvoice/8
European Commission 2005. "Plan D for Democracy, Dialogue and Debate"., COM(2005) 494 final, Brussels: European Commission.
Folketinget. 2015. *Diskussionsoplæg til konference om udvalgsarbejdet,* February 4. Copenhagen: Folketinget.
Hartley, J. 2005. "Innovation in Governance and Public Service: Past and Present." *Public Money and Management* 25 (1): 27–34.
Hartley, J., E. Sørensen, and J. Torfing. 2013. "Collaborative Innovation: A Viable Alternative to Market Competition and Organizational Entrepreneurship." *Public Administration Review* 73 (6): 821–830. doi:10.1111/puar.2013.73.issue-6.

Helms, L., Ed. 2012. *Poor Leadership and Bad Governance*. Cheltenham: Edward: Elgar.
Hendriks, C. M. 2013. *Research Report: Elected Representatives and Democratic Innovation*. Canberra: Crawford School of Public Policy.
Hofstad, H., and J. Torfing. 2016. "Collaborative Innovation as a Tool for Environmental, Economic and Social Sustainability in Regional Governance." *Scandinavian Journal of Public Administration* 19 (4): 49–70.
Hood, C., and M. Lodge. 2006. *The Politics of Public Service Bargains: Reward, Competency, Loyalty – Blame*. Oxford: Oxford University Pres.
Kenis, P., and V. Schneider. 1991. "Policy Networks and Policy Analysis: Scrutinizing a New Analytical Toolbox." In *Policy Networks*, edited by B. Marin and R. Mayntz, 25–59. Frankfurt-am-Main: Campus Verlag.
Kingdon, J. W. 1984. *Agendas, Alternatives, and Public Policies*. Boston: Little Brown.
Klijn, E. H. 2014. "Political Leadership in Networks." In *The Oxford Handbook of Political Leadership*, edited by R. A. W. Rhodes and P. 'T Hart, 403–418. Oxford: Oxford University Press.
Kooiman, J., Ed. 1993. *Modern Governance*. London: Sage.
Koppenjan, J. F. M., M. Kars, and H. V. D. Voort. 2009. "Vertical Politics in Horizontal Policy Networks: Framework Setting as Coupling Arrangements." *The Policy Studies Journal* 37 (4): 769–792. doi:10.1111/j.1541-0072.2009.00334.x.
Lijphart, A. 2012. *Patterns of Democracy: Government Forms and Performance in Thirty-Six Countries*. New Haven, CT: Yale University Press.
Marsh, D., and R. A. W. Rhodes, Eds. 1992. *Policy Networks in British Government*. Oxford: Oxford University Press.
Meier, K. J. 2000. *Politics and Bureaucracy: Policymaking in the Fourth Branch of Government*. Fort Worth, TX: Hartcourt College Publishers.
Mezirow, J. 2000. *Learning as Transformation: Critical Perspectives on a Theory in Progress*. San Francisco, CA: Jossey Bass.
Nye, J. S. 2010. "Power and Leadership." In *Handbook of Leadership Theory and Practice*, edited by N. Nohria and A. Khurana, 305–332. Boston, MA: Harvard Business Press.
OECD. 2013. *Government at a Glance 2013*. Paris: OECD.
Osborne, D., and T. Gaebler. 1993. *Reinventing Government*. Reading: Addison-Wesley.
PAC. 2012. *Report on the Economics of Energy Generation*. Sydney: Legislative Assembly of the NSW Parliament.
Parry, K. W., and A. Bryman. 2006. "Leadership in Organizations." In *The Sage Handbook of Organization Studies*, edited by S. Clegg, C. Hardy, T. Lawrence, and W. Nord, 447–468. London: Sage.
Polsby, N. W. 1984. *Political Innovation in America: The Politics of Policy Initiation*. New Haven, CT: Yale University Press.
Rittel, H. W. J., and M. M. Webber. 1973. "Dilemmas in a General Theory of Planning." *Policy Sciences* 4 (2): 155–169.
Sabatier, P. A., and H. C. Jenkins-Smith. Eds. 1993. *Policy Change and Learning*. San Francisco, CA: Westview Press.
Skelcher, C., and J. Torfing. 2010. "Improving Democratic Governance through Institutional Design: Civic Participation and Democratic Ownership in Europe." *Regulation & Governance* 4 (1): 71–91. doi:10.1111/rego.2010.4.issue-1.
Sørensen, E. 2006. "Metagovernance: The Changing Role of Politicians in Processes of Democratic Governance." *The American Review of Public Administration* 36 (1): 98–114. doi:10.1177/0275074005282584.
Sørensen, E., and J. Torfing. 2015. *Beskrivelse Af Formålet Med Og Indholdet Af Den Nye Politiske Arbejds- Og Organiseringsform*. Gentofte: Gentofte Kommune.
Termeer, C., and S. Nooteboom. 2014. "Innovative Leadership through Networks." In *Public Innovation through Collaboration and Design*, edited by C. Ansell and J. Torfing, 170–187. London: Routledge.
Torfing, J. 2016. *Collaborative Innovation in the Public Sector*. Washington, DC: Georgetown University Press.
Torfing, J., B. G. Peters, J. Pierre, and E. Sørensen. 2012. *Interactive Governance: Advancing the Paradigm*. Oxford: Oxford University Press.
Tucker, R. C. 1995. *Politics as Leadership*. Columbia, MO: University of Missouri.

United Nations. 2015. *The Millennium Development Goals Report.* Accessed June 25, 2016. http://www.un.org/millenniumgoals/2015_MDG_Report/pdf/MDG%202015%20rev%20(July%201).pdf

Warren, M. E. 2002. "What Can Democratic Participation Mean Today?" *Political Theory* 30 (5): 677–701. doi:10.1177/0090591702030005003.

Workman, S., B. D. Jones, and A. E. Jochim. 2009. "Information Processing and Policy Dynamics" *The Policy Studies Journal* 37 (1): 74–92.

ㆆ OPEN ACCESS

The challenge of innovating politics in community self-organization: the case of Broekpolder

Jurian Edelenbos, Ingmar van Meerkerk and Joop Koppenjan

ABSTRACT
This article explores whether political innovations are realized in introducing community self-organization in local government and which role conflicts local politicians may experience. We conducted an in-depth, longitudinal case study of a citizen initiative to investigate if it resulted in the emergence and consolidation of new roles and practices for politicians. The case study shows that politicians had difficulty in adopting new roles, and eventually fell back to more traditional roles. Explanations found in the case are the historically grounded structure of the political system, the incompatibility of roles, a lack of boundary spanning leadership in the political arena and the lack of trustful relationships. It turns out that the adoption of innovative roles by politicians to accommodate innovate governance practices in the context of community self-organization is difficult and provides a key challenge for those pursuing such innovations.

Introduction

This article deals with whether and how the introduction of community self-organization in local governments contributes to the emergence of political innovations. In many European countries (but also in other countries around the world), municipalities experiment with new ways of community engagement that goes beyond regular (government-induced) participation (Edelenbos 2005; Torfing et al. 2012). In these processes of community self-organization local governments remain at a distance, leaving more freedom for citizens to develop, decide and implement local plans and projects (Boonstra and Boelens 2011; Van Meerkerk, Boonstra, and Edelenbos 2013).

The introduction of community self-organization can be approached as a push-factor to innovation, demanding new roles, not only for citizens and public administrators, but also and especially for politicians (Sørensen and Torfing 2007). As explained in the introduction to this special issue, innovation can be understood as intentional developments and realizations of new ideas and implies some form of discontinuity of existing structures and practices (Sørensen, introduction to this special issue). However, whether community self-organization will result in

This is an Open Access article distributed under the terms of the Creative Commons Attribution-NonCommercial-NoDerivatives License (http://creativecommons.org/licenses/by-nc-nd/4.0/), which permits non-commercial re-use, distribution, and reproduction in any medium, provided the original work is properly cited, and is not altered, transformed, or built upon in any way.

politicians taking up new roles is still an open question, as many barriers from existing representative democracy system can hamper the innovation.

Our main goal in this article is therefore to investigate to what extent and in what way the introduction of a specific community self-organization (the 'Federation Broekpolder') resulted in exploring, taking up and consolidating new roles by elected politicians in the municipal council, and which factors are important in explaining the level and nature of political innovation.

Theoretical framework

Community self-organization and political innovation

Citizen engagement in public policy and policy implementation can be deliberately initiated by governments. Governments organize and set the rules and roles for citizens to participate in policy-making and decision-making (Irvin and Stansbury 2004; Roberts 2004). However, citizen engagement can also be initiated by citizens themselves. Several authors argue that this specific form of interactive governance is on the rise in many liberal democracies (e.g. Bang 2009; Dalton 2004; Marien, Hooghe, and Quintelier 2010). They reflect new forms of civic engagement, which can be labelled as self-organization (Nederhand, Bekkers, and Voorberg 2016; Van Meerkerk 2014; Boonstra and Boelens 2011).

In this contribution we approach community self-organization as a specific and new form of interactive governance that has implications for governmental structures, processes and institutions (Edelenbos and Van Meerkerk 2016). Community self-organization has implications for actors in the government system, especially politicians. Some argue that new democratic models evolve when citizens become more actively engaged in policy-making and decision-making (Klijn and Skelcher 2007).

Three different models of democracy

The introduction of citizen self-organization in local governance practices brings along institutional implications for representative democracy (Edelenbos 2005; Sørensen and Torfing 2007). In this section we discuss three models of democracy: representative, participatory and self-organizing democracy. We don't take any normative stance, but approach these three forms as ideal types, that will be used as heuristic tools to identify political innovations: the invention, adoption and consolidation of new roles by politicians.

In the *representative form of democracy* the electorate votes for parties or individuals on the basis of policy packages and programmes. In this view, democracy is seen and approached as essentially a decision-making procedure, with the democratic political system as a machine for resolving issues – an 'issue machine' (Braybrooke 1974). In this model various traditional perspectives on democracy are merged: democracy as an effective procedure to arrive at collective decisions, democracy as a safeguard for citizens from government hegemony, and democracy as an expression of the will of the people.

In *a participatory view of democracy* vocal citizenship is considered important and government feels the urge and need to activate citizens in the policy- and decision-making. In a participatory democracy citizens get the opportunity to take part in the process of policy- and decision-making, being able to represent their own views and interests and influence the development and choice solutions in an open process of deliberation (Pateman 1976).

In *a self-organizing view of democracy* also active and vocal citizenship is considered important, but in a different relationship to government (Fung 2003; Hirst 1994). Self-organizing democracy strongly resembles associative ideas on democracy in which human welfare and liberty are both best served when as many of the affairs of a society as possible are managed by voluntary and democratically self-governing associations (Hirst 1994). In contrast to the representative and participative model of democracy, citizens develop their own power to prepare, develop and implement decisions, plans and projects. In this way, bottom-up initiatives of empowered and highly educated citizens emerge today, that no longer are initiated, conditioned and controlled by government (Marien, Hooghe, and Quintelier 2010; Van Meerkerk, Boonstra, and Edelenbos 2013). Self-organizing democracy is broader than the notion of direct democracy as it is not only about providing opportunities for referenda or petitions. Citizens in a self-organizing democracy have opportunity to act and implement plans and ideas by themselves, and can be approached as 'citizen control' on the participation ladder (Arnstein 1969). This self-organizing democracy is also different than participatory democracy, in which governments determine under which conditions and rules citizens can participate. In a self-organizing democracy citizens have the initiative and (co)determine for a large part under which conditions their participation takes place. The self-organizing democracy model is also different than the protective democracy model (MacPherson 1979), as the latter is focused on protecting material wealth and maintaining a free market. Moreover, broad-based civic engagement is discouraged in this model unless it is related to protecting civil liberties. The self-organizing democracy has an explicit focus on an active civil society and an active stance for government in facilitating and stimulating bottom-up initiatives.

New roles for politicians and role dilemmas

The three different models of democracy imply different roles for politicians. We suggest that the introduction of citizen self-organization will push politicians towards self-organizing democracy and towards exploring and adopting new roles that constitute this practice.

In the representative democracy model elected representatives hold the primacy of politics meaning that politicians hold the power to decide; decision-making is done in the political arena that consists of representatives of different political parties (Held 2006). The elected state, provincial or municipal council is the only body that is allowed to speak and to act on behalf of the people (representative role), the highest in hierarchy in the municipal organization (regulating and governing role), and the supervising unit to which the executive is accountable (controlling role). In this latter role the council assesses whether decisions correspond to earlier agreements. This central position is considered logical as citizens in turn hold politicians accountable for the action taken by the government (Held 2006; MacPherson 1979).

In the participative democracy model the representative role is less prominent as citizens will directly represent their interests, values and perspectives. However, politicians as meta-governors set the conditions and rules under which participation takes place, which is referred to as a framework-setting role (Sørensen and Torfing 2007; Koppenjan, Kars, and van der Voort 2011). Politicians are supposed to 'create, monitor, and steer interactive governance arenas in which they themselves may or may not participate' (Torfing et al. 2012: 152). They set the rules and procedures for participation processes and give purpose and direction to interactive processes by defining objectives, provide funding and set up procedures for monitoring and evaluating the outcomes (Sørensen and Torfing 2007). Next to framework setting, Torfing et al. (2012) also distinguish direct participation as a 'hands-on' form of meta-governance in which politicians are actively and directly involved in interactive policy arenas, trying to influence the policy agenda in dialogue and negotiation with other stakeholders.

In the third model of self-organizing democracy, politicians fulfil yet different roles, since the democratic principles of this model stresses autonomy, local ownership and self-regulation (Fung 2003; Hirst 1994). But also in this model, interaction with governmental institutions is necessary and self-organizing democracy is not approached as a substitute for representative democracy, but as a supplement to it (Hirst 1994). First, elected politicians can take up a role in anticipating which subjects and fields of community initiatives may be worthwhile. At the same time, politicians get a more responsive role, responding to civic initiatives, in which citizens propose ideas for more civic responsibility. Moreover, politicians also actively discuss the potential drawbacks in citizen initiatives, as these may exclude certain groups and individuals (Sørensen 2006), and in this way safeguard potential vulnerable social groups and their interests and values. In addition, politicians may create conditions that are favourable for citizens to start and to sustain these self-organizing initiatives (by providing financial resources, assistance by experienced and knowledgeable civil servants, loosening stringent formal procedures and rules, etc.). Facilitation takes place with less emphasis on reaching a certain result or outcome (as within framework-setting in the participative democracy model), but by creating a favourable context and supportive conditions for self-organization. In this view, politicians provide room and create niches in which civic initiatives can evolve. Sørensen and Torfing (2007) call this process management as one of the meta-governance strategies in which politicians help to reduce tensions, empower particular actors and lower the transaction costs of networking by providing different kinds of material and immaterial resources. This then also touches upon their third role in a self-organizing democracy: procedural monitoring. This is related to the first role (safeguarding democratic values) and refers to their more process oriented role in policy and decision-making. In a self-organizing democracy, politicians have a far less content wise role in formulating public policies and providing policy directions, but have a more important role in monitoring the process and procedure through which deliberation between different societal groups and self-organization of communities take place. In this, they can monitor whether key democratic values are not violated and can provide procedural directives by which inclusion of relevant stakeholders or the citizenry in general, transparency and accountability are realized (cf. Hirst 1994; Torfing et al. 2012).

Table 1 summarizes, in an ideal type categorization, the roles of politicians as envisioned by the three democratic perspectives that underlie the practices of traditional government, participation and community self-organization. In practice role

Table 1. Ideal type roles of politicians in different democracy models.

Representative democracy	Participative democracy	Self-organizing democracy
Representation	Framework setting	Anticipation and safeguarding public values
Regulation and governing	Debating and direct participation	Stimulating and facilitating
Control and accountability	Monitoring	Procedural monitoring

conflicts may occur: when politicians taking up roles that do not match the characteristics of the governance practice at hand, as they don't know which role is appropriate in certain circumstances, combine incompatible roles or unintentionally navigate between roles in an unpredictable way. It may also be that during the case politicians experience dilemmas with regard to taking up specific roles, given contradictory implications. For instance when stimulating and facilitating citizen initiatives, they may fear for their ability to take independent decisions at the end of the day as prescribed by representative democracy. But when they stay aside, they might miss opportunities to facilitate innovative democratic practices and to influence their direction. So politicians may be reluctant to get involved in participative processes, reasoning that they should not become committed and should keep their hands free to take the ultimate decisions. However, taking this stance, they are also 'in danger of losing their ability to control what is going on, to make qualified and informed decisions, and to gain support fort their political programme among relevant and affected stakeholders' (Torfing et al. 2012, 155).

In this contribution to the special issue, we investigate whether politicians explore, take up and consolidate new roles in dealing with the emergence of a community self-organization and which drivers and barriers influence the emergence and consolidation of these innovations.

Research methodology

In this article we use insights from a specific case study. The case study is about Federation Broekpolder (multipurpose area development) in the Dutch municipality of Vlaardingen. This case study is an example of a most likely case, which is one that, on all dimensions except the dimension of theoretical interest, is predicted to achieve a certain outcome (Eckstein 1975). The logic of most likely case design is based on the inverse Sinatra inference – if I cannot make it there, I cannot make it anywhere (Levy 2002, 442). So in our study we selected Broekpolder as a most likely case as it is a far-reaching example of community self-organization to which the local government developed a stimulating stance and policy. Therefore, we expect that political innovation will happen because of this in general positive and receptive attitude of the municipality. If political innovation won't take place here, then it is unlikely that it occurs elsewhere.

During this period from 2007 to present, we obtained information at different momentums. We conducted frequent interviews (every year, starting in 2008) with key informants (leading citizens and a civil servant). Furthermore, we conducted semi-structured interviews with a broader set of stakeholders in the case: politicians, civil servants, and aldermen. Next to the interviews, we analysed relevant documents, such as reports of council meetings, policy documents (white papers, memos) and evaluation reports of the governance experiment. Lastly, we observed several meetings organized by the Federation in which new governance arrangements with the local government and other stakeholders were discussed. This longitudinal study enabled us to acquire an in-depth understanding of the initiative, how politicians responded and which roles they took in the process.

As earlier indicated we use the models of democracy and the roles that are derived from these models as sensitizing concepts, heuristic tools to identify political innovations and to guide our analysis (Bowen 2008).

Case analysis: what happened in innovating politics?

Case study: introduction

The case is about a political innovation in which citizens propose to turn traditional roles of policy- and decision-making around. It concerns a citizen initiative in the city Vlaardingen, a city of around 70.000 inhabitants in the province South Holland. In 2002 the local community (residents, local politicians and local societal organizations) opposed to plans by the provincial government (the province of South-Holland) to designate the Broekpolder area as a search location for 'rural living', and to build country houses. The Broekpolder area is an old recreational area of approximately 300 hectares in the north-western part of the city. This plan caused protests of ten thousand people who signed a protest letter. The province responded by postponing action to realize rural housing, on the condition that the recreational and natural value of the area would be increased. In 2010, the area would be evaluated again by the province.

This threat of housing in the area triggered a group of citizens to take initiative for mobilizing other citizens and users of the area to develop ideas for increasing the recreational and natural quality of the area. Furthermore, they also proposed a governance experiment, aimed at turning the roles of government and citizens upside down: citizens would get an initiating and leading role in the policy- and decision-making process instead of politicians, executives and civil servants. Local politics was – at that time – characterized by deadlocks and lacked a clear vision about the future of this area, which was an important motive for proposing this governance experiment. The group of citizens in close contact with a civil servant and an alderman developed a white paper in which their proposed innovation was further elaborated. In Figure 1, their proposed governance model is visualized. The citizen group was recognized as community self-organization and formalized on 5th October 2006 in the Foundation Federation Broekpolder.

In Figure 2, a short overview of the process in different rounds is displayed. We use these different rounds (Teisman 2000) to describe and analyse the evolution of the interaction process between the citizen initiative and the local council. For each round we examine to what extent political innovations emerged by looking at the roles politicians took up and what drivers of and barriers to role changes can be identified.

Roles of councillors in the civic initiative

Round 1 (2002 to January 2006): the 'governance experiment'

In close contact between a civil servant and an alderman, the citizen group further developed their white paper to develop a new governance model in which the roles of government officials, politicians and citizens were innovated. This citizen initiative

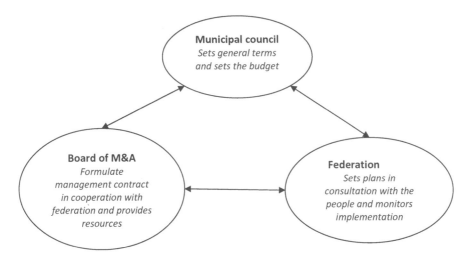

Figure 1. The proposed governance model developed by the group of citizens.

was coined as 'governance experiment Federation of users Broekpolder' and was discussed in a council meeting in January 2006.

The discussion in the council meeting shows that council members were reluctant to transfer responsibilities towards the citizen initiative. Before the council came to a decision, several questions concerning the future roles, tasks and responsibilities of both citizen group and council were raised and addressed to the initiators of the experiment and a discussion among councillors took place. Several council members expressed their uncertainty about the future role of the council. To what extent would the council still be involved in the decision-making process concerning the Broekpolder area? Implementing such projects was politically sensitive in the Broekpolder area, where competing political interests were at stake. For example, some council members feared '*making a decision from which they could not withdraw later on*', as one councillor expressed. The council was afraid of losing its grip on the citizen initiative that could lead to accomplished facts. Some councillors wanted '*clear rules*' provided in advance. The whole council was reluctant '*to create an extra organizational layer that could not be democratically controlled*', as one councillor argued. Lastly, some critical questions were raised about the representativeness of the Federation. The strong involvement of some prominent Labor Party (PvdA) members in the initiative caused scepticism among some other political parties.[1]

Despite a reluctant and critical attitude, the white paper was approved by the council with a large majority. The experiment fitted well with the ambition of the coalition that time to stimulate citizen participation. This ambition was explicitly mentioned in the coalition agreement (2006–2010). Furthermore, the council requested the Board of Mayor and Aldermen to further elaborate this experiment in close cooperation with the citizen group and to look for additional funding. The council also made some clear statements when approving the citizen initiative: '*the council should keep control*' and '*at all times financial transparency and feasibility should be constantly assessed*' (Municipality of Vlaardingen 2007, 1).

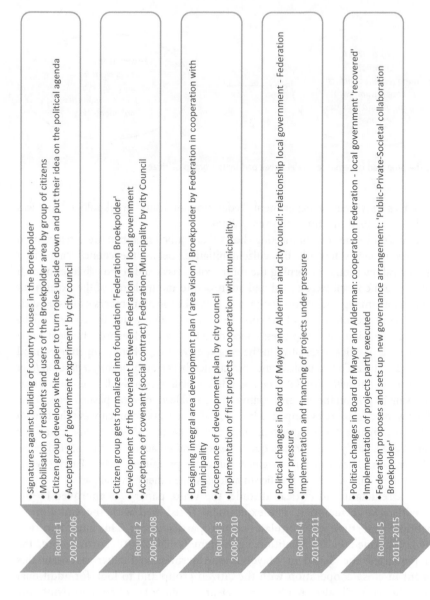

Figure 2. Overview process case citizen initiative Broekpolder.

Hence, in this first round, (a large majority of) the council supported the citizen initiative and white paper, but was generally reluctant to change its traditional role and to delegate decision-making power to the citizen initiative. Councillors struggled with the dilemma of giving room for this governance experiment and letting some of their responsibilities go versus staying in the lead, stressing their controlling role. They generally stuck to their traditional roles of being in the lead and in control, a main aspect in the representative democracy model.

Round 2 (2006–2008): the covenant between federation and local government

After the approval of the governance experiment in January 2006, the citizen group had the task to further elaborate the governance experiment in cooperation with the Board of Mayor and Aldermen. They came up with the idea to develop a covenant to formalize agreements and conditions concerning the extent and form of citizen initiative. In close contact with a civil servant these conditions were further elaborated. In this respect, different levels of citizen engagement were proposed. These are the following (in sequence of increasing influence): (1) *qualified advice* regarding daily area management issues, (2) *co-production* and *binding advice* regarding small area developments, but also initiating proposals and (3) taking a *leading, initiating role* in developing large plans and projects for the area (self-organization), within settled frameworks, and *co-production* of the management of these projects. The citizen group also wanted a small budget for their organization and for developing plans for the area.

Regarding the communication and deliberation with the council and Board of Mayor and Alderman, the citizen group proposed to meet once a year with the responsible council committee, once a year with the Board of Mayor and Alderman and four times a year with the responsible Alderman. Furthermore, the Federation proposed the creation of a so called 'political portal' which aims '*to make communication and interaction [with the Council] easier and aims to increase the quality and the speed of decision-making*' (Municipality of Vlaardingen 2007, 1). By this political portal the citizen group wanted to secure political embedding of the citizen initiative in order to accelerate the decision-making process and to ensure a timely alignment with politics on specific project proposals. As noted in the proposed covenant:

> If some ideas are beginning to show maturity in the Federation or if council members like to raise something, then an orientation meeting between Federation and (parts of) the city council can take place. These meetings are informal in the sense that the Council' members are free to bring their ideas. (Municipality of Vlaardingen 2007, 6)

In the spring of 2007, before the covenant was discussed in the council, the Federation organized a role game with the council and the Board of Mayor and Aldermen in order to jointly experiment with the new roles and to address the questions and uncertainties which were raised during the council meeting in the first round. As the president of the Federation notes, this was meant to '*show what the consequences would be of working with [the proposed model in the covenant]*'. This took away some of the concerns of council members. As one council member notes: '*Subsequently there was a search for which role every party [council, Board, administration, Federation] would get. [...] This role play was a true "eye opener" for the future situation. It also took away some uncertainty and reluctance among council members.'*

The covenant was subsequently discussed in a council meeting in November 2007. Some councillors raised critical concerns regarding the power delegated to the federation according to the proposed levels of participation. Again, critical concerns were raised concerning the representativeness of the citizen group and its network. This led to a small adjustment in the covenant: the Federation should make enough effort to bring all the interested parties and stakeholders together that reflect the population of Vlaardingen. The Federation got a budget, approved by the council, for their organization and the maintenance and development of the area. The Federation was bound by this budget, by the overall structure plan for the region and by legal requirements.

Within the council, the political portal was debated fiercely. Eventually the council didn't agree upon supporting this idea. The political parties had insufficient confidence in each other to create this portal. *'Who can we trust to represent the council in this portal?'*, stated one council member. Another council member noted: *'The formation of this political portal was politically too sensitive. Every party wanted to participate in this portal'*. Next, the council wanted to maintain the freedom and opportunity to have the final say at the end of the policy process, as they always had. They did not want to prematurely commit themselves to certain unofficial agreements or statements. In all, it was decided to operate in accordance with the traditional political procedures to deal with project proposals; that the council would be involved via the responsible Council committee on spatial planning and would be informed by the Municipal Board on this issue. Some council members noted that early involvement with the citizen initiative and its activities would also lead to politicisation of the public debate.

Next to the rejection of the political portal, the council adopted a motion that requested an adaptation to the covenant. This motion stressed the importance of making first a joint vision (by co-production of Federation and local government), which has to be approved by the council and which can serve as a framework in which requirements for the future plans and projects developed by the Federation were expressed. This motion was a result of the discussion among councillors that the Federation might develop all kinds of projects which would not fit with their political vision (programme) of the area.

Thus, in this second round, councillors generally stuck to their controlling role (central in the representative democracy model), but they also took a framework setting role (central in the participative democracy model): the covenant is accepted, a budget is allocated and a vision document is requested. This document would function as a framework to assess the progress in the Federation. In this round we also observe that councillors were reluctant to take a direct participating role (participative democracy model): they rejected the idea of the political portal. Two important reasons for this rejection were the will to keep room for political manoeuvring (preventing early commitment) and a lack of trust to allow certain councillors to take seat in the portal. In this round, the role dilemma of staying independent versus participating came to the fore: councillors feared that this portal would negatively influence their independent position and their regulating and controlling role. If something is discussed and approved in the portal by a selective number of participating councillors, the general committee has nothing to say and decide anymore.

Round 3 (2008–2010): development of a joint vision

In this round the Federation had the task of developing a formal vision (so-called Integral Area Development and Maintenance Plan), in co-production with the local government, to (re)develop and maintain the area. In this round, the Integral Plan was prepared and developed by prioritizing a couple of projects and plans: development of a core nature area, archaeological educative centre, activity forest, and a small harbour.

In this round, the citizen initiative was discussed a couple of times in the city council. They urged that this area development and maintenance plan, which was being developed internally in the Federation, included representative support from a broader set of citizens of Vlaardingen. In line with previous comments of the council concerning the representativeness of the Federation, being dominated by specific active citizens (see Rounds 1 and 2), they requested a 'support poll' and 'participation procedure' for citizens who were not directly involved in the Federation. The chairperson of the Federation took up this amendment by opening up the planning process and by following a formal public consultation procedure. The council approved this approach and this public consultation procedure and 'support pole' was implemented in close co-operation with the local government. The Federation used this formal consultation procedure at the same time to introduce itself to a broader audience and to mobilize (potential) engaged citizens and volunteers for their organization. They invited citizens explicitly to react on the concept vision and polled the level of support for the specific plans in the vision document.

After successfully completing these activities, the council approved the integral area plan. After this approval, the interaction between Federation and council is mainly characterized by informing – in line with the covenant. At this moment in time, some councillors were still not well-informed about the role and activities of the Federation. Furthermore, some political parties expressed their concern about the way plans are developed out of sight of the council. They feel at a distance without chance to monitor and control the activities towards the development of the Broekpolder area.

Just as in the previous rounds, the council took mainly a controlling role (following the representative democracy model). They demanded a 'representation check' related to the integral area development plan to control whether the plans are supported by a larger public in the municipality. In this role they expressed their concerns about the representativeness of the Federation Broekpolder. In this round, the council also opted for a monitoring role, in which they get informed about the results and new plans for the area development. Given the substantive nature of this monitoring role, it matches the participative democracy model. However, councillors didn't take an active attitude in gathering information about the progress and issues regarding the citizen initiative.

Round 4 (2010–2011): political pressures

In the fourth round (April 2010 to June 2011), the council elections took place. The result was that Labor Party got halved (from twelve to six representatives in the

Council) and the local political party (Livable Municipality) grew from three to six representatives. As a result, a new alderman from this political party was appointed in the Board of Mayor and Aldermen, and was held responsible for the Broekpolder dossier. This party was already very reluctant to the emergence of the Federation Broekpolder and this was expressed by the new alderman. One of first things he did was to re-allocate the budget for the Broekpolder, making it no longer exclusive. He put this allocated money into a general budget for green area development. This made it harder for the Federation to get its ideas financed by the municipality. The projects came to a halt, and the chairperson (and the general board) of the Federation started looking for additional funding, primarily from the regional government, in order to move ahead with plans. The coordination and interaction between the local government and the Federation strongly decreased in this round.

In this round there was almost no direct interaction between Federation and council. The political climate changed in the council and a larger part was now less interested and committed to the citizen initiative. Directly after the election, the Federation put lots of time and energy to get the new elected council members informed about the Federation (its goals and progress). They also pointed out their displeasure concerning the budget cuts. Later on the Federation informed the council about the decrease of attention and involvement of the local government regarding the business of the Federation. The council took notice of this signals and complaints, but remained largely indifferent and didn't take any action in this matter.

Thus, in this fourth round, the council took a passive, marginal controlling role. There was no monitoring of the activities of the Federation or the relationship with the local government. The council approved the budgetary restrictions, but did not take a controlling role in keeping the Board and/or the Federation to their agreements as laid down in the covenant. For instance, the covenant was not followed by the Board concerning the participation and consultation agreements (Partners and Pröpper 2011). Other roles of the council are not observed in this round. The citizen initiative slipped the attention of the Council after re-elections when a new council was constituted.

Round 5 (2011–2015): towards a public–private–society partnership

At the beginning of the fifth round (Spring 2011), the new alderman of Livable Vlaardingen who didn't fancy the Federation much, had to leave due to political affairs, and again a new alderman was appointed. This alderman from the Green Party was more supportive towards the Federation. Interactions between the Federation and the municipality were revitalized. This connection was further strengthened when the civil servant who was active in the first two rounds was reassigned as 'programme manager – participation' in order to develop a strategic political role on participation and self-organization. The alderman, programme manager participation and the regional manager Broekpolder looked for renewed interaction with the board of the Federation. However, budgetary problems remained. The Federation kept looking for broader connections with private and public organizations to get a public–private–society partnership arranged in which different organization show commitment (financially or in other ways) to the citizen initiative. The municipality of Vlaardingen has become one of the partners of the Federation. In this way, citizen participation has turned into *government participation* in the Federation Broekpolder. The Federation continuously searched for ways to innovate government and politics by forming a public–private–society partnership.

After the 2014 elections, the composition of the council changed again (with decrease of party Livable Municipality and increase of Socialist Party and status quo of Labor Party). Furthermore, both at the national and the local level, the discourse of the 'Participation Society' (compare: Big Society in the UK) had gained prominence and became part of the new coalition agreement. As a result, the general attitude of the council towards the Federation changed in the sense that the federation got compliments and support for what they achieved and for what they were doing. Generally, they took a supportive and reactive stance. In the council committee on spatial panning, they noted that they follow the new developments with interest, that they understand the new situation (that the federation is exploring a new governance arrangements and want to professionalize more), and that they wait how this is going to develop. Although the council took a positive stance, it remained at a distance and was not closely involved in the business of the Federation. The council was also absent in the discussion about the possible changing role of the municipality in the public–private–society partnership.

Hence, in this final round, we observe again a rather passive role of the council: the council gets informed, but did not take a participating or monitoring role. Council members firmly stuck to the traditional roles of the representative democracy model, but in a rather passive way.

In Table 2, the different roles politicians took during the life cycle of the citizen initiative are summarized. Furthermore, the various role dilemmas are summarized. In the next section we are going deeper into the identified drivers and barriers.

A closer look at political innovations, drivers and barriers

What are the findings on the occurrence of political innovations and the emergence of innovative role fulfilment by politicians in the case?

First of all, during the case various political innovations were developed and proposed to allow politicians to take up new roles that would facilitate the citizen self-organization. One of the innovations discussed was the political portal, an innovative arrangement that would facilitate politicians to directly participate in debates with citizens and members of the Federation and monitor the community self-organization. However, this portal was not realized since politicians feared it would jeopardize the exercise of their traditional representative and controlling roles. Instead of adopting a role that would fit self-organizing democracy, politicians stuck to their traditional role as prescribed by the model of representative democracy.

A second innovation concerned an agreement on innovative role fulfilment, as laid down in the covenant that was agreed upon between the Federation and the city council. A third innovation involved the request to the Federation to develop a vision that could function as a framework. However, the specific roles that were suggested in these two latter innovations and especially the idea of framework setting and the monitoring of substantive results rather match the model of the participative democracy than that of the self-organizing democracy. It seems that the council and council members treated the initiative as if it was a form of traditional citizen participation. The request to the citizen group, requiring them to take the lead in the planning process and strengthen their representativeness by involving other citizens can be

Table 2. The roles of politicians and role dilemmas in the case citizen initiative Broekpolder.

Round	Political innovations; fulfilment of new roles?	Drivers and barriers
1 (2002–2006)	Politicians stick to traditional, representative roles	Drivers • Political support and active involvement of politicians in debates • Active role of citizens as catalysts coming up with innovative proposals • Collaboration between citizens and alderman and civil servant, who acted as boundary spanners Barrier • Role conflict between supporting the initiative by letting go versus the urge to stay in control
2 (2006–2008)	Rejection of the idea of a political portal that would arrange direct participation of politicians; adoption of covenant with new roles that match participative democracy	Driver • Political support and active involvement of politicians in debates • Active role of citizens as catalysts coming up with innovative proposals • Collaboration between citizens and alderman and civil servant, who acted as boundary spanners Barriers • Role conflict between direct participation and taking independent decisions • Role conflict between steering in substance and process • Political competition in the traditional representative democracy arena
3 (2008–2010)	Politicians request substantive vision and framework, give citizens the lead in planning and require proof of representativeness. Partly matches roles of participative and self-organizing democracy	Driver • Political support and active involvement of politicians in debates Barrier • Role conflict between steering in substance and process
4 (2010–2011)	Politicians hardly monitor. Roles match the representative democracy model.	Barriers • Support for initiative disappears. • No direct participation
5 (2011–2015)	Politicians hardly monitor. Roles match representative democracy	Barriers • Support for initiative returns, but politicians stay at distance • No catalyst role of citizens

seen as unorthodox and a fourth political innovation that actually matches the model of self-organizing democracy.

Although at the end of Round 2 the covenant was signed and the framework was set, councillors didn't consolidate this role. In the next rounds they did not ask for information needed to fulfil their monitoring and controlling role effectively. Here we see that political innovations which were adopted were not fully carried through and implemented in practice. Even when the majority of politicians were supportive to the community self-organization and cooperative governance arrangements with it, they felt back to traditional roles of non-participation and controlling, as suggested by the model of representative democracy. Although political innovations were suggested and adopted on an ad hoc basis, the process did not result in innovations that were implemented and institutionalized.

Looking for explanations we first turn to drivers behind the political innovations that emerged in the various rounds of the case. First, as far as ideas for political innovations were brought forward, they were developed by the citizen group in close collaboration with the involved alderman and the civil servant of the municipality. The latter two acted as boundary spanners in facilitating, consolidating and embedding the citizen initiative within the municipal organization (see also Van Meerkerk 2014). Although politicians initially were involved in discussing these new ideas, they did not came up with them themselves, nor did they further developed them.

Second, although the leadership as provided by the alderman that was supportive of the federation and a driving force behind the idea of the portal and the covenant, seems to have been important, it apparently was not enough to get political innovations implemented and institutionalized. Certainly the change in leadership due to the electoral cycle provides an explanation for this, although the reestablishment of supportive leadership later on did not result in political innovations to be carried through.

A third driving force can be found in boundary spanning processes such as the role play in which citizens and council members engaged. This role play proved to be supportive in developing a common understanding and mutual trust between these politicians and citizens participating in the Federation. It contributed to a receptive climate in which the innovative proposals could be discussed. However, these learning impacts took place in niches and were not strong enough to overcome the centrifugal dynamics of the political process within the municipality and the disruptive impact of the electoral cycle.

The case study provides ample information on barriers to political innovations, and more specifically to the adoption, implementation and institutionalization of the new roles as foreseen in the model of self-organizing democracy. A first barrier consisted of the role conflicts that evolve as a result of politicians, operating within the setting of representative democracy, getting involved in practices of self-organizing democracy. The latter requires the taking up of new roles that are hard to combine with traditional roles, politicians want or need to fulfil simultaneously. So the idea of the portal was rejected since councillors feared that some of them – participating in the portal – might get an information advantage as compared to the others. At other occasions a more participative role was considered to be at odds with the political primacy requiring politicians taking decisions in an independent way and to be able to fulfil a controlling role. Generally, politicians were reluctant to get closely involved. However, later on in the process (Round 3), councillors complained about a lack of information and a lack of involvement, with the result that they were not able to fulfil their framework setting and monitoring role. We see a clear tension between getting well-informed versus keeping an 'independent' position (monitoring versus staying independent). However, this independent position makes it difficult to have a steering and framework setting role. Each potential new role of politicians (monitoring, debating) might come at the expense of their traditional controlling role (primacy of politics). In the end, these role conflicts and dilemmas led to a fallback to the familiar patterns and roles of the representative democracy model.

A second barrier, and related to the difficulty politicians experienced in dealing with the Federation, was the erratic relationship between the citizen group and local politicians in the municipal council. In the first rounds of the interaction process, politicians were still involved in the debates on which role they should fulfil in dealing with the Federation. But gradually their involvement became less, and eventually their relationship with the citizen initiative was characterized by the absence of interaction and trust, which doesn't provide a fertile ground for political innovation.

Besides the role conflicts and the lack of interaction and trust, the disruptive impact of the electoral cycle proved to be important. As a result of the change in the political power balance, the willingness to take up new roles that were supportive for the development of the federation disappeared. From that moment onwards the implementation and institutionalization of the political innovation were no longer part of the political agenda. What was more, even when the political climate became more favourable again, the conditions for political innovation proved to be dramatically changed. Earlier the efforts on the side of the Federation to build relationships with councillors and involve them in their plan, had been a major driver behind these innovations. Now, citizens had become aware of how vulnerable investments in these relationships were, and developed strategies to decrease their dependencies of politicians and the municipality. Due to these process dynamics, the policy window for political innovations that with a lot of effort was created during the first rounds of the interaction process, no longer was open.

Conclusions

Our first observation is that community self-organization succeeded as a governance experiment in community self-organization, but failed as an attempt to innovate political practices. New and productive relationship between members of the community self-organization and the municipal organization, civil servants and Mayor and Aldermen, emerged in the governance experiment. However, new relationships with and new roles for the politicians didn't come about. The council approved the experiment, it discussed new roles, took efforts in applying these, but eventually fell back upon its traditional representing and controlling roles.

How can we explain this unexpected outcome? We deliberately picked a case in which there are plausible reasons to expect political innovation to occur. The case study therefore provides us with interesting insights about why political innovation, in the context of community self-organization, is so difficult to get anchored. Reflecting on the different drivers and barriers we found, we see two different types of explanatory factors: one concerns the characteristics of the (current) political system and the second concerns (management) implementation issues. The first holds that innovation in politics is hard, because the political system is strongly based on partisan tradition. Party-political debates for votes and power play hamper finding a safe surrounding (niche) in which innovation is explored and implemented (cf. Peters 2010). In our case study, this political competitive climate among the political parties and its members didn't provide a fertile ground for experimentation and political innovation.

The second type of explanatory factors is related to management implementation issues. As far as ideas for political innovations were brought forward, they were developed by the citizen group. Although politicians initially were receptive to these new ideas, they did not came up with or further developed these themselves. According to the literature innovation needs collaborative efforts of various actors involved (Sørensen and Torfing 2011). However, there was a lack of boundary spanning leadership embedded in the political arena (cf. Van Meerkerk 2014). Politicians did not actively contribute to the invention of innovations and eventually redrew from this collaborative effort.

At the same time, these two different types of explanation can be argued to be related (in this case). It can be argued that a lack of boundary spanning leadership in the political arena is caused by the partisan nature of the political system. The latter stimulates confrontation and distinction and doesn't foster cross-boundary activities and coordinating mechanisms to facilitate political innovation. Further study is needed to explore these two types of explanation and their mutual relationship. In general further research is needed to examine whether these conclusions can be confirmed in other cases and/or in different political and democracy systems.

Reflecting on the theoretical democracy models and accompanying roles of politicians we proposed, it may well be that the roles we suggested in our theoretical section are too much conflicting, not appropriate or even unrealistic. The case study shows that politicians are multi included in practices of representative democracy and self-organization. The roles these practices prescribe, are not simply complementary. This results in tensions, for instance when councillors decide to engage in debates with citizens of the federation, but fear commitments since according to the representative democracy model they need to be able to take independent decisions at the end of the day. This requires navigating between for example representative and facilitative roles (see also Torfing et al. 2012). This is not only difficult due to the tensions between the various roles, but also because politicians don't have the experience and/or skills that serve as a compass to navigate, and/or don't find a safe and stimulating political environment to experiment.

Lastly, the case provides indications how to improve the conditions for political innovation. Enhancing the role of drivers in pursuing political innovation, such as facilitating interaction, the presence of boundary spanning leadership, the fulfilment of the role of catalyst, and boundary spanning processes, are important guidelines for action. In addition we have seen the niche nature of these initiatives and their instable environments as important barriers for political innovations. Avenues to deal with that can be sought in activities that further the implementation, institutionalization and upscaling of these innovations: for instance by enhancing learning processes across initiatives, building networks between citizen self-organizations and with front-running municipalities, signalling out political innovations that can be seen as best practices, and seeking support from authoritative institutions to propagate these practices. Future research should not only be aimed at further clarifying the types of political innovation that are supportive to citizen self-organizations, but also at the contextual conditions that enhance the opportunities to realize these political innovations.

Note

1. This led the Federation to involve more people with other (political) backgrounds (such as the VVD, the liberal party).

Disclosure statement

No potential conflict of interest was reported by the authors.

References

Arnstein, S. R. 1969. "A Ladder of Citizen Participation." *JAIP* 35 (4): 216–224.
Bang, H. P. 2009. ""Yes We Can": Identity Politics and Project Politics for a Late-Modern World." *Urban Research & Practice* 2 (2): 117–137. doi:10.1080/17535060902979022.
Boonstra, B., and L. Boelens. 2011. "Self-Organization in Urban Development: Towards a New Perspective on Spatial Planning." *Urban Research & Practice* 4 (2): 99–122. doi:10.1080/17535069.2011.579767.
Bowen, G. A. 2008. "Grounded Theory and Sensitizing Concepts." *International Journal of Qualitative Methods* 5 (3): 12–23.
Braybrooke, D. 1974. *Traffic Congestion Goes through the Issue-Machine: A Case-Study in Issue Processing, Illustrating a New Approach*. London: Routledge/Thoemms Press.
Dalton, R. J. 2004. *Democratic Challenges. Democratic Choices. The Erosion of Political Support in Advanced Industrial Democracies*. New York, NY: Oxford University Press.

Eckstein, H. 1975. "Case Studies and Theory in Political Science." In *Handbook of Political Science*, edited by F. Greenstein and N. Polsby, 79-138. Vol. 7. Reading, MA: Addison-Wesley.

Edelenbos, J. 2005. "Institutional Implications of Interactive Governance: Insights from Dutch Practice." *Governance* 18: 111-134. doi:10.1111/gove.2005.18.issue-1.

Edelenbos, J., and I. F. Van Meerkerk, eds. 2016. *Critical Reflections on Interactive Governance. Self-Organization and Participation in Public Governance*. Cheltenham: Edward Elgar Publishers.

Fung, A. 2003. "Associations and Democracy: Between Theories, Hopes, and Realities." *Annual Review of Sociology* 29: 515-539. doi:10.1146/annurev.soc.29.010202.100134.

Held, D. 2006. *Models of Democracy*. Cambridge: Polity Press.

Hirst, P. 1994. *Associative Democracy. New Forms of Social and Economic Governance*. Cambridge: Polity Press.

Irvin, R. A., and J. Stansbury. 2004. "Citizen Participation in Decision Making: Is It Worth the Effort?" *Public Administration Review* 64 (1): 55-65. doi:10.1111/puar.2004.64.issue-1.

Klijn, E. H., and C. K. Skelcher. 2007. "Democracy and Governance Networks: Compatible or Not?" *Four Conjectures and Their Implications, Public Administration* 85 (3): 1-22.

Kooiman, J., ed. 1993. *Modern Governance. New Government-Society Interactions*. Newbury Park: Sage.

Koppenjan, J. F. M., M. Kars, and H. van der Voort. 2011. "Politicians as Meta-Governors. Can Metagovernance Reconcile Representative Democracy and Network Reality?" In *Interactive Policy Making, Metagovernance and Democracy*, edited by J. Torfing and P. Triantafillou, 129-148. Colchester: ECPR Press.

Levy, J. S. 2002. "Qualitative Methods in International Relations." In *Millennial Reflections on International Studies*, edited by M. Brecher and F. P. Harvey, 432-454. Ann Arbor: University of Michigan Press.

MacPherson, C. B. 1979. *The Life and Times of Liberal Democracy*. Oxford: Clarendon Press.

Marien, S., M. Hooghe, and E. Quintelier. 2010. "Inequalities in Non-Institutionalised Forms of Political Participation: A Multi-Level Analysis of 25 Countries." *Political Studies* 58 (1): 187-213. doi:10.1111/post.2010.58.issue-1.

Municipality of Vlaardingen. 2007. "Bestuurlijk Experiment Participatie Broekpolder." Nota aan B&W. [White paper]. Vlaardingen: Municipality of Vlaardingen.

Nederhand, J., V. Bekkers, and W. Voorberg. 2016. "Self-Organization and the Role of Government: How and Why Does Self-organization Evolve in the Shadow of Hierarchy?" *Public Management Review* 18 (7): 1063-1084.

Partners and Pröpper. 2011. *De Broekpolder in ontwikkeling. Evaluatie van de samenwerking tussen de gemeente Vlaardingen en de stichting Federatie Broekpolder*. Noordwijk: Partners and Propper Advies.

Pateman, C. 1976. *Participation and Democratic Theory*. Cambridge: Cambridge University Press.

Peters, B. G. 2010. "Bureaucracy and Democracy." *Public Organization Review* 10 (3): 209-222. doi:10.1007/s11115-010-0133-4.

Roberts, N. 2004. "Public Deliberation in an Age of Direct Citizen Participation." *The American Review of Public Administration* 34 (4): 315-353. doi:10.1177/0275074004269288.

Sørensen, E. 2006. "Metagovernance the Changing Role of Politicians in Processes of Democratic Governance." *The American Review of Public Administration* 36 (1): 98-114. doi:10.1177/0275074005282584.

Sørensen, E., and J. Torfing. 2011. "Enhancing Collaborative Innovation in the Public Sector." *Administration & Society* 43 (8): 842-868. doi:10.1177/0095399711418768.

Sørensen, E., and J. Torfing, eds. 2007. *Theories of Democratic Network Governance*. London: Palgrave Macmillan.

Teisman, G. R. 2000. "Models for Research into Decision-Making Processes: On Phases, Streams and Decision-Making Rounds." *Public Administration* 78: 937-956. doi:10.1111/padm.2000.78.issue-4.

Torfing, J., B. G. Peters, J. Pierre, and E. Sørensen. 2012. *Interactive Governance. Advancing the Paradigm*. Oxford: Oxford University Press.

Van Meerkerk, I. 2014. *Boundary Spanning in Governance Networks: A Study about the Role of Boundary Spanners and Their Effects on Democratic Throughput Legitimacy and Performance of Governance Networks*. Rotterdam: Erasmus University Rotterdam.

Van Meerkerk, I., B. Boonstra, and J. Edelenbos. 2013. "Self-Organization in Urban Regeneration: A Two-Case Comparative Research." *European Planning Studies* 21 (10): 1630-1652. doi:10.1080/09654313.2012.722963.

Political parties and innovation

Carina S. Bischoff and Flemming Juul Christiansen ⓘ

ABSTRACT
Public innovation and political parties are usually not studied together. Given the key position parties hold in representative democracies, it is somewhat odd that their influence on public innovation has not been explored. We propose to open this line of inquiry and introduce a typology that highlights four avenues for studying the links between public innovation and political parties: linkage, programme, interaction and policy. We use the typology to discuss relevant themes and empirical examples in existing literature and to formulate of a number of hypotheses about innovation of political parties themselves as well their impact on potentially innovative public decisions. One major expectation is that hierarchical parties with centralized leadership make more efficient decisions but that sustainable innovation outcomes promoted by collaborative efforts are easier to obtain for decentralized political parties with participatory internal democratic processes.

Introduction

In representative democracies, the public policies that we may characterize as either innovative or conservative are ultimately adopted by the elected representatives of political parties, whose impact on innovation in the public sector is a promising area for research. The political 'backdrop' (i.e. the conditions) for innovation in the public sector is constituted by the way in which organizational actors such as political parties structure themselves, and the extent to which they incorporate innovative ideas (see Sørensen, 2016). The term 'innovation' was originally applied in analyses of economic competition between private companies. Over the past decades, however, it has entered research on public sector, notably to describe developments in policy fields, processes and governance networks (Schumpeter 1934; Kettl 2002; Kooiman 2003; Sørensen and Torfing 2011; Voorberg, Bekkers, and Tummers 2015; De Vries, Bekkers, and Tummers 2016).

A key concern is to understand the drivers and barriers to innovation with an eye to increasing the capacity or efficiency of the public sector. However, as discussed by Sørensen in this issue, the literature on innovation in the public sector has largely neglected the political level, focusing instead on the administrative branches of government and policy (though see Helms 2016 for a recent exception to this trend). This strong focus on the output side, in Easton's terms, leads to neglect of political 'input' in the form of public demands (and support) and thereby of democratic politics in general. This is somewhat paradoxical given that the innovation literature recognizes that forms of democratic decision-making constitute important conditions for public innovation (Røste 2005).

Sørensen refers to numerous studies that show how political parties have become increasingly detached from, and irrelevant for, citizens; and inquire into how this can be compensated for, including how political parties may be bypassed in a more participatory or activist democracy. Helms (2016) critically discusses a number of suggested innovations in democratic decision-making, including referendums, term limits and new forms of direct participation by citizens, such as participatory budgeting (Helms 2016).

Our aim in this article is different. We refrain from a priori dismissing the role of political parties in innovation. Instead, we provide a systematic overview of the conditions that can influence whether political parties, autonomously or through their interactions, can become sources of change and innovation. This is because we consider that political parties remain key actors in modern democratic representation: come Election Day, voters essentially face a choice between competing political parties. Between elections, parties are the principal actors in organizing legislative and oversight processes in parliament. Moreover, they form the governments that initiate the vast majority of the bills passed by parliament, and they implement the policies adopted. The democratic process essentially provides political parties with the key to gaining office and to acting as possible 'policy entrepreneurs' in adopting innovative policies (Polsby 1984; Minstrom 1997; Zons 2015). According to Helms (2016), political parties are often agents of innovation and change.

Innovation is not just something that political parties can 'enact' in policy. It is also something they are expected to engage in themselves. Political parties are under constant pressure to renew their organizations, policy platforms and leadership in order to remain competitive in the electoral arena and to achieve other key goals such as influence over policy, office or internal democracy (Harmel and Janda 1994). New parties, as well as the changes and adaptations effected in existing parties' organization and ideology, may be conceived as innovations in themselves, and they may also affect the conditions for innovative policies on the output side.

In our article, we relate the concept of innovation to the literature on political parties, and develop a number of relevant research themes and tentative hypotheses. Notably, we seek to clarify how the concept of 'innovation' is related to the terms 'party' and 'party system change'. Our particular focus on political parties means that we do not address reforms of the democratic institutions themselves, such as those mentioned above (cf. Helms 2016). Neither do we study primarily non-partisan providers of civil society linkages, such as interest groups, social movements, media or governance networks; nor other institutional actors such as constitutional courts, local governments or public bureaucracies or agencies.

After defining our key concepts, we develop a theoretical typology for 'Parties and Innovation' that distinguishes between the form and content of partisan representation, both for individual parties and for their interaction in party systems. Aided by that typology, we identify research themes and possible hypotheses that require further empirical study. We develop four thematic areas for studies of representational innovation: namely, (i) organizational forms and (ii) ideological platforms of individual parties, as well as (iii) patterns of government and policy formation and (iv) ideological dimensions in party systems. First, we look at the main features of these four themes and discuss general trends and innovations within each, drawing primarily on examples from the Western European context. Second, we discuss which features may influence policy outputs and innovations in these. Finally, we discuss how different democratic models that combine various characteristics from each quadrant may create different expectations for party-driven policy change and innovation. We recognize that the 'causal chain' from the abstract features we discuss to the actual output is complex. We therefore see this work as a first step towards theorizing the relationship between parties and policy innovation rather than a conclusive statement.

Towards a typology of political parties and innovation

Concepts of representation and innovation

Sørensen argues in this issue that innovation may take place in polity, politics and policy. Where polity refers to the institutional level, politics involves processes and policy involves output. Using this conceptual framework, our article focuses on 'processes', with a particular emphasis on political parties. 'Polity' – i.e. institutions – influences the actions and interactions of parties, just as we expect parties to influence output. For a clear and meaningful discussion of these topics, we first need to define the concept of innovation as it can be brought to bear on the topic of political parties in their individual and collective roles.

There is an ongoing debate about what kinds of phenomena can rightly be classified as innovative, and the term itself has proven to be somewhat elusive. De Vries, Bekkers, and Tummers (2016) point out that 'novelty' as well as 'adoption of an idea' are the two most frequently used definitions of public sector innovation. The most commonly cited definition in the field is by Rogers (2003, 12), who defines innovation as '*an idea, practice or object that is perceived as new by an individual or other unit of adoption*'. Sørensen and Torfing (2011), on the other hand, define it as '*an intentional development and realization of new creative ideas*'. By making 'perceptions' and 'intentionality' critical to defining an innovation, both definitions preclude changes in output or process that are not the result of a conscious reflection by the involved actor(s) from being characterized as innovations.

The following discussion draws on an extensive literature on party and party systems and changes in these (see Mair 2006). The type of intentional new developments we can call 'innovations' only really occur at the level of the 'agent', i.e. the individual party. New developments at the systemic level – for instance in types of interaction or the degree of polarization in policy positions – are often the unintended consequences of uncoordinated actions by different actors. System-level characteristics and developments are, however, equally important to how the political system performs. One important parameter of this performance is the capacity for passing policy. The system-level properties and changes in them must therefore form an integral part of the analysis. New developments at this level will be referred to as changes rather than innovations. However, it is important to remember that while unintentional changes at the system level cannot be classified as 'innovations', they may influence the conditions for passing innovative policies.

Naturally, the relationship between parties and institutions is not one-way. Parties are in the privileged position that they can change the rules of the game. However, changing key institutional rules – typically those defined in constitutions – requires

Table 1. Typology of party innovation.

	FORM	CONTENT
PARTY	'LINKAGE'	'PROGRAMME'
PARTY SYSTEM	'INTERACTIONS'	'POLICY '

super-majorities and sometimes referendums. If the bar is set so high that rule change is beyond the immediate reach of parties, such institutions can be treated as exogenous to party behaviour. Others, like electoral laws, may be more endogenous as well subject to manipulation by, parties as part of the political process (Benoit 2004) but, as stated above, we leave institutions out of our analysis.

In Table 1 we present a typology of party innovation. It draws on Pitkin's (1967) distinction between 'actors' (representatives) and 'content' (what is being represented) that is widely used in analyses of democratic representation. The typology comprises four quadrants, each referring to key aspects or areas of democratic agency that can influence its behaviour and output, including innovative policies. The typology neither explains nor predicts anything in itself. Instead, it serves as an important classification tool in the ensuing analysis and discussion of political parties and innovation. The categories are fairly broad but we will focus on the features of political parties that are likely to have implications for the policy-making process and output of the system.

The two dimensions of the typology are: (i) the two levels of agency – party and party system; and (ii) the form versus content dimension of representation. While individual parties are the bedrock of the representational system, understanding the dynamics of representation requires an analytical level beyond the individual party. As party scholars have pointed out, the party system is more than simply the sum of the parties that constitute it, and it should therefore be conceptualized as important in its own right (e.g. Sartori 1976; Mair 2006). The party system is essentially defined by the competitive, conflictual or collaborative interactions of the parties that constitute it (e.g. Bartolini 1999, 2000). In two-party systems, of which there are in reality very few left (Mair 2006, 55–56), the interaction is so simple and antagonistic in nature that we need hardly consider it. However, in multiparty systems which are the present-day norm in advanced democracies, interaction patterns are critical in defining how voters are represented and how the system works. Party system change modifies the options for voters and often implies a change in modus operandi. Hence, Table 1 distinguishes between 'party' and 'party system' as different levels of representation where change can occur, and that can have implications for policy output.

The second dimension in the typology concerns the 'form' versus 'content' aspect of representation. The 'form' dimension captures the organizational and process aspects of representation; while the 'content' dimension refers to the political substance i.e. the values, policies, decisions, instruments, etc. The form and content dimensions play out in different ways at the level of the party and the party system.

In the following, we discuss change and innovation in each of the four quadrants in turn, and relate their characteristics and overall trends and changes in these to the likelihood of policy change and innovation.

Linkage

The first field combines 'party' with 'form' and is entitled 'LINKAGE' in the typology. The term reflects our focus on the organizational traits and processes in political parties that link them not only to voters, as normally done in the literature on parties, but also to other actors such as think tanks, unions and other interest organizations, or even the state itself (cf. Lawson and Merkl 1988). The importance of these links lies in the potential role they play for key decision-making processes in political parties that may influence the policy-making capacity of the political system. Parties are organized in different ways that influence how they connect with civil society and state actors, as well as the extent to which they do so. A number of organizational traits – such as how parties recruit candidates, select leaders, obtain resources and adopt policy programmes, etc. – are critical to how they perform their functions.

Change in this quadrant can occur when new parties enter or when established parties undergo organizational changes. We would argue that entry of a new party only constitutes an innovation in 'linkage' if the party represents something new in terms of its organizational characteristics – not if it merely offers a new label for structures already present in the system. What counts as an important innovation in party organization? The literature on party organizational change provides examples of such developments in a number of descriptive party types. An evolutionary trend can be seen when older party types are rendered obsolete by a new political context and new, more viable types. The virtual disappearance of the elite/cadre party type in the late nineteenth and early twentieth centuries is a classic example of this. Unable to meet the challenges posed by mass enfranchisement and the subsequent mass mobilization of the electorate under the aegis of the 'mass-party' type, the individualistic elite parties that lacked organizational roots in civil society gradually disappeared (Katz and Mair 1995; Duverger 1954). The new, mass party type was a membership organization embedded in a particular class or segment of society. Candidates were recruited among the membership and typically worked their way up to leadership positions. The Social Democratic parties represented the mass party in its purest form but former elite parties of the right wing partly emulated this organizational structure in what has been termed a 'contagion from the left' (Duverger 1954). The heyday of the mass party type also came to an end with the emergence of post-industrial society from the 1960s onwards, which challenged its foundations. Traditional identities and ideologies waned and partisan loyalty declined with them; voters started to withdraw from parties as members and also became less predictable on Election Day, while new values and political priorities emerged. The mass party model has therefore been challenged by new forms more suited to navigating the political waters in a post-industrial/post-modern political context: namely, the 'catch-all' party, 'electoral-professional party' or the 'cartel party' to mention some of the most cited types (see Krouwel 2006 for overview). Some of the most salient organizational features of these models are: top-down decision-making, a more independent leadership vis-à-vis the party organization, recruitment of candidates with media appeal instead of loyal party 'soldiers', and professionalization of the party bureaucracy. The cartel party type is further characterized by withdrawal from civil society in favour of increased dependence on the state (Katz and Mair 1995). The environment (primarily the electorate) is typically conceived as the main driver of changes in party organization, although internal dynamics in parties can also play a role. Harmel and Janda's (1994) theory of party change proposes that change arises through the interplay of parties' 'primary goals' and changes in their environment (i.e. changes that challenge their ability to attain their primary goals). The salient primary goals discussed are the 'usual suspects': obtaining votes, getting into office and policy/ideology advocacy. This argument is theoretically compelling. If a party aims for government office, events leading to non-attainment of this goal are likely to cause reforms in the party. The same event is unlikely to have much of an effect on a party that aims to achieve policy influence or advocacy, however.

Krouwel (2006) divides the key organizational characteristics dealt with in party typologies into four main dimensions. The first two concern the organizational foundations of the party that can be closer to the *state or to civil society* and draw on *individual or collective resources*. Furthermore, parties can be described in terms of their internal decision-making processes as *hierarchical with a strong top-down centralized control* or *horizontal, open and democratic*; and their organizational characteristics may be labelled either *professional (and capital-intensive)* or *amateur and volunteer-based*; and finally their leadership recruitment patterns may be categorized as *open and inclusive* or *closed and elitist*. We consider that these key organizational characteristics are helpful when discussing innovation in party organization, and when linking party organization to outcomes.

The question is: what implications do these organizational features have for the ability of parties to respond to complex societal problems and pass innovative policies to address them? Helms (2016) argues for bringing political leadership 'back in' in studies of innovative decision-making. If leadership does indeed matter, then we might expect features such as centralized control and top-down decision-making to be important in parties. A key issue is whether party leadership is constrained by the party organization or whether it has room for manoeuvre on questions of policy. Resources can also play a role here, as dependence on powerful interests – i.e. a party's (in)dependence on resources – might constrain the leadership just as much as internal factors. We might therefore hypothesize that party types featuring stronger top-down decision-making structures, and which draw on collective rather than individual resources, are in a better position to lead policy innovation than parties where leadership is constrained by internal democracy or by dependence on powerful external actors. In other words, an organization that has few veto players is more flexible in its positions and better able to alter the status quo. A dominant trend in party organization is the tendency for power to be concentrated in the leadership. This 'presidentialization' not only of the prime minister's position but also of the party leadership (Webb, Poguntke, and Kolodny 2012) might enable parties to take the lead in policy innovation. However, while leadership may be a necessary precondition for change and innovation in policy, we would argue that it is not sufficient on its own. The leadership must be properly motivated to pursue such an agenda for this to happen, and this may depend partly on the incentives to do so and partly on the motivations and convictions of the leader.

Helms (2016) also offers a different perspective, namely that 'wicked' problems require collective or shared leadership. Involvement, information sharing and active deliberation among different actors are important for coming up with policy proposals that address difficult problems. This would suggest that parties with horizontal, open and democratic decision-making would fare better in this regard. Other dimensions, such as candidate recruitment, can also play a role in the internal deliberation processes. Strong competition between candidates within the same party at election time may undermine the sharing of information and ideas and could therefore be detrimental to developing new policy ideas within the party. However, selection of candidates by the national party leadership would constitute a form of centralized control. It may be that recruitment patterns which curb internal competition and privilege political expertise over media savvy can also contribute to the policy-making capacities of the party itself. Finally, parties that have stronger connections to civil society and seek input from experts and relevant stakeholders in policy formulation should also have better chances of formulating more policy proposals with a sustainable effect on policy outcomes.

To investigate whether party organization plays a role in party policy formulation, we believe that the entry of 'Green' as well as 'right-wing populist' parties in much of Western Europe offers interesting cases for study (Mair and Mudde 1998). The Green parties tend to emphasize 'grassroots' forms of internal party democracy, whereas the right-wing populist parties are often dominated by charismatic leadership figures (Frankland, Lucardie, and Rihoux 2008; Van der Brug and Mughan 2007). In the Danish People's Party that entered Parliament in 1995, for instance, we find a strong centralization of power in the leadership. At the opposite end of the organizational scale, a new green party – the Alternative – entered Parliament in 2015. It was launched in 2013 and at that time featured only a few key values and aims, inviting the population to participate in the formulation of its political programme through a series of 'political laboratories' open to all those interested in participating. The Alternative has already played a role in proposing and passing new policies. Both parties represent innovations in 'linkage' and we also suggest that they would represent interesting cases for a comparative analysis of the role of party hierarchy in policy-formulation in political parties.

Programme

The next quadrant at the party level addresses what the parties stand for, which is summarized by the term 'PROGRAMME'. We think of it as more than the collection of concrete policy suggestions that a party may make in or out of office. It also relates to the political identity of a party and typically includes some form of broad ideology or vision for society that underpins and connects the specific policies proposed. It regards the party as a 'carrier of ideas' (Vassallo and Wilcox 2006) that often draws directly or indirectly on one of the classic ideologies, i.e. liberalism, conservatism or socialism (Heywood 2012).

There are considerable differences between parties with respect to how fully developed or detailed their ideology is (Klingemann et al. 2006). Some parties are equipped from the outset with a relatively coherent set of ideas about politics, society and the economy; while others arise in response to a single problem or issue and lack a broader ideational platform. Even if a coherent ideology linked to a policy programme may be a high bar to set, it is common for parties in electoral manifestos to present a broader socio-political narrative or message, and not simply rely on a collection of specific proposals to convince voters to support them. Changes in a party's views can occur at different levels and take many forms. Perhaps the most fundamental form of innovation is in a party's ideology or fundamental narrative, as such changes may have wide-ranging and long-lasting implications for tangible policy proposals and behaviour.

The next level to look for new developments is in the area of concrete policy goals and policy proposals. New combinations of policy items could also be considered innovative, such as the 'new winning formula' of some populist right-wing parties, which combines rightist immigration with centrist economic policies (De Lange 2007). Furthermore, even when parties tend to agree on a wide range of topics when they communicate to voters, real disagreements on priorities could become evident in the emphasis that parties place on different topics (Green-Pedersen 2007).

How do ideologies or basic values espoused by political parties have an impact on the likelihood of changes in actual policy proposals and positions? Parties with very 'strong' and distinct ideologies on the left or right with clear narratives and visions for society are perhaps less likely to adopt new policy proposals and more likely to stick with the 'status quo' than adopt pragmatic changes of policy. On the contrary, parties with broader and vague ideational platforms in the ideological centre of the party system are perhaps more likely to change direction in policy and adopt new proposals. Nevertheless, radical parties may cause change by affecting the position of mainstream parties. An example of this is when centre-right parties take up more critical positions towards immigration and the European Union as a result of pressure from right-wing populist parties (Hooghe and Marks 2008, 121–122).

Interactions

The third quadrant is at the level of the party system. As Sartori (1976) argued, the essence of the party system is the pattern of INTERACTIONS between parties. Competition and cooperation within party systems influence voters' choice (or lack of it) of alternative governments at election time, as well as which parties are relevant to policy-making processes and outputs, and what incentives the parties have to respond to electoral views and interests (Bartolini 1999, 2000).

In most established democracies, party interactions follow relatively stable and intelligible patterns. These may, however, be interrupted from time to time and in a few rare cases even be completely recast as old systems collapse. In the literature there is an ongoing debate about how to conceptualize, classify and register party systems and changes in them. As one of the leading scholars in the field comments, the key problem in these analyses is that change 'is seen as either happening all the time or scarcely happening at all' (Mair 2006, 63).

The search for classification schemes is closely linked to the expectation that certain features can predict how the system will perform in terms of government – and even regime – stability and efficacy. Scholars in the field have identified broad numerical categories such as two-party, two-and-a-half or multiparty systems on the basis of simple or qualified (e.g. relevance or size) counts of parties (Duverger 1954; Blondel 1968). More finely tuned approaches based on a formula that combine numbers with relative vote shares into a score for 'the effective number of parties' have been widely influential (Laakso and Taagepera 1979). The belief that the number of parties predicts working properties such as stability and efficacy is the key to this effort. Sartori (1976), however, added extra – qualitative – features in his influential classification scheme, which combines the numerical 'format' of a party system with its ideological properties (the extent of polarization in ideological positions) in the expectation that the two dimensions were intimately related and would also interact to influence system performance. Thus, the system would either incentivize competition for the political centre or for the political extremes (fewer parties would curb polarization, while more parties would do the opposite) with obvious consequences for the working properties of the system as a whole (cf. the section on 'Policy').

The notion that a lower number of parties would enhance the stability and efficacy of the system has influenced the choice of electoral systems in, for instance, the Fifth French Republic in 1958, as well as the Second Republic in Italy following the corruption scandals in the early 1990s, which directly aimed to reduce the number of political parties (Bartolini, Chiaramonte, and D'Alimonte 2004). Nevertheless, the number of parties alone does not determine outcomes. Although the paradigm cases of unstable governments had high numbers of parties (the Weimar Republic and the French Fourth Republic), many other countries like the Netherlands, Switzerland and Sweden provide strong evidence to the contrary. While two-party systems may have higher efficacy – i.e. be more productive in terms of policy output that departs from the status quo – multiparty systems with broad coalitions may take longer to produce legislation, but there is no evidence that they are less effective in dealing with a wide range of economic and social problems (see Lijphart 1999). Multiparty systems may, in fact, produce stability in the realm of policy over time if many parties and even oversized majorities are involved in policy-making.

A more recent look at party systems suggests that we should not be overly concerned with numbers, but focus directly on the pattern of interactions. Mair (2006) presents three key 'working' properties related to patterns of government formation – i.e. the collaborative and competitive patterns observed – in the party system rather than their structural features.

The first is whether government participation is potentially open to all parties in the system or limited only to some while excluding other parties. Many party systems have 'pariah parties' that are not considered as potential partners either in forming government or in policy-making. This has mostly applied to parties on the extreme left or right (Sartori 1976; Bale 2003). Particularly large 'pariah parties' seriously affect patterns of alternation in government.

The second dimension pertains to the use of *new* or *old well-known formulas* in the composition of government, and directly concerns innovation in government. It can occur when new parties take up government office; when established parties do so for the first time; or when parties that have not joined forces before agree to collaborate in forming a government. Occasionally, parties join a government for the first time, like the Progress Party in Norway in 2013 or the Greens in Sweden in 2014. With the exception of Switzerland, where the same four parties have formed governments almost without interruption ever since 1959, most countries do experience changes in the composition of parties in government. Sometimes, major breakups occasion a complete rupture with the past. Examples include Italy in the 1990s, and more recently countries heavily affected by the economic crisis such as Greece, Spain, Iceland and Ireland where new patterns of interaction replace old, well-known ones.

The third dimension concerns *the pattern of alternation*, notably whether there is one at all, and if so whether it is wholesale or only partial. This is critical to whether voters can hold political parties in office accountable. Wholesale alternation implies that all incumbent ministers are replaced by ministers from other parties. This pattern is typical in two-party systems but also in multiparty systems where parties collaborate to form two competing blocs, as often occurs in the Scandinavian countries (Christiansen and Damgaard 2008). Alternation can also be partial, which is more typical of countries with broad coalitions that include more parties than they need to gain a simple majority, as is often found in Finland or in countries where centrist parties play an important role, as with the Christian Democrats in Italy, the Netherlands before the 1990s, or the FDP in Germany (Green-Pedersen 2004). In party systems where minority government is common, patterns of cooperation with opposition parties are also important (Christiansen and Damgaard 2008).

Based on the discussion above, we now propose a number of hypotheses that relate the properties of party systems to the making of policies that produce significant change.

First, we propose that systems featuring fewer parties in a governing or policy-making coalition should, *ceteris paribus*, create better conditions for passing legislation that departs from the status quo than systems consisting of many parties. There are, simply, fewer differences to consider. This resembles the basic proposition in veto-player theory (Tsebelis 2002). A high number of actors able to block legislation can prevent policy changes, which is the reason for legislative gridlock in the US Congress (Binder 1999). On the other hand, more actors – potentially representing different stakeholders and segments in society – can help create deep and sustainable solutions, which is the argument supported by Lijphart (1999). The search for new solutions may, in fact, be spurred by the difficulty of reconciling different positions – as long as it does not lead to deadlock. We might therefore expect lower legislative output, but also more innovative solutions, the greater the number of actors involved.

The literature on coalition governance suggests that institutional solutions can help parties to enter agreements despite trust and delegation issues (Strøm, Müller, and Bergman 2008). Coalition agreements, inner cabinets and junior ministers can aid in the creation of new and possibly controversial policies that might otherwise be difficult to pass if parties used them in electoral competition. Despite the individualized rational choice perspective that characterizes this literature, it does point to ways to incorporate collaborative efforts in finding joint, innovative solutions to policy problems. We hypothesize that policies agreed to with the framework of coalition governance arrangements are more likely to be innovative both in content and outcome.

Secondly, alternation in government is likely to play a role by influencing parties' incentives to respond to electoral interests. Parties that do not live with the threat of being ousted have few incentives to make great efforts to pass major pieces of legislation in response to social or economic problems. However, parties need a reasonable time horizon in office in order to develop legislative bills – aided by the bureaucracy – that can be passed in parliament. With very short time horizons, we might also expect parties to be less willing to risk passing policies that imply major departures from the status quo.

Finally, the entry of a new party into government, or a new configuration of older parties in a governing coalition, could well hold the greatest potential for introducing the greatest number of new policy changes. However, as discussed in the 'linkage' and 'programme' sections above, new parties or constellations are not necessary preconditions for new policies. Changes within existing parties, such as a new leadership or changes in organizational form, may just as well bring about changes in direction and new forms of collaboration.

Policy

The final 'quadrant' in the typology is the content dimension of the party system that we here simply refer to as 'POLICY'. As discussed in the previous section, party systems can be characterized by properties such as the number of parties in them and how they interact, but what the parties stand for creates a policy space that sets the parameters for possible policy outcomes. This policy space can be described in two main terms: the degree of polarization, and the type and number of policy dimensions (Hunt and Laver 1992). The degree of polarization describes how far from each other the political ideologies and policy programmes proposed by parties in the same system are. As already mentioned, an archetypical example of a highly polarized party system is the Italian one which, in the whole post-war period until the 1990s, included a large communist party on the extreme left and a smaller fascist party on the extreme right. In this case, government and policy-making was left in the hands of one major and a number of minor centre parties with no viable alternative majorities that could challenge them. The degree of polarization does not just come down to the question of differences in fundamental ideologies but also the extent to which these positions actually preclude political dialogue that can identify common ground and negotiate compromises when it comes to day-to-day policy matters. When polarization is strong, positions are typically perceived as 'fundamental principles', and even as a matter of personal identity, and as such they cannot easily be trifled with. The other aspect is the conflict dimension. In most Western European party systems, the left–right dimension fundamentally deals with economic questions of free market versus state intervention and the redistribution of wealth. Other conflict dimensions have played – and still do – a significant role in a number of countries, namely centre–periphery divides, church–state relations or authoritarian–libertarian ('social control') values. According to Lipset and Rokkan (1967), the European party systems arose from the twin revolutions of nation state building and the industrial revolution. These cleavages organized political life and made it predictable so that the party systems of the 1960s were, according to some, 'frozen' along the conflict lines of the 1920s (Lipset and Rokkan 1967). In the second half of the twentieth century, the foundations for some of these conflicts – such as class consciousness or religious affiliation – weakened, while new issues entered the political agenda, such as emphasis on democratic participation, the environment and climate, the EU, and globalization, etc. (see Warwick 2002). Some of these issues – such as the environment – have to a large extent been aligned with the old left–right conflicts, with left-wing parties adopting greener agendas. Others, such as issues of EU membership, globalization and also immigration, have not been so easy to fit into the old axes of conflict, thereby causing tensions within the party system (Green-Pedersen 2007). For historical reasons related to socialist ideology, the political left adopted so-called 'anti-authoritarian' stances and the political right was therefore left with the task of being 'tough on crime' and 'opposing immigration', etc. There is no inherent logical connection between the economic and the authoritarian dimensions, but this historical bias has meant that the combination of economically left-wing policies with authoritarian political policies has proven not to be a realistic option in most countries. Even when majorities do exist on certain policies, they may not become political reality due to the constraints imposed by the process of government formation (Laver and Shepsle 1996). On the other hand, new types of policy may arise from new majority constellations as well as existing coalitions responding to outside pressures. The coalition between Conservatives and Liberals in the United Kingdom between 2010 and 2015 allowed for certain policies that would not have been possible without this particular combination of parties. The universal welfare states of the Nordic countries were also largely a result of compromises between social democratic and agrarian parties as a response to the economic crisis of the 1930s (Esping-Andersen 1985).

There is no doubt that both the extent of polarization and dimensions matter in terms of the types of policy output that we can expect from a political system, but under what circumstances can we expect any systematic relationship?

A precondition for innovation, defined as the 'intentional realization of new ideas', is that the political system is able to make effective decisions about major policy areas. Polarization can reduce this capacity. When extreme positions are integral to the actors' identities (and relationship to their voters) it may prove impossible to engage in pragmatic dialogue with a view to solving common problems. Hence, the system need not shut down as has been the case in the 'dysfunctional' and 'gridlocked' political system of the United States in recent years where major reforms like the Obamacare health reform have become rare occurrences (Binder 1999, 2015). However, the result of such a situation may also be that the political centre is forced to act alone – as occurred, for instance, in Italy in the period before the 1990s – or for the executive to fill out the decision-making void administratively.

The dimensionality of the policy space could affect policy change and possibly policy innovation by political parties. Based on a single dimension, the median position represents a majority, party actors in proximity to each other will tend to collaborate, and changes in policy will imply compromises between them that are likely only to lead to incremental changes – close to the median for the system – rather than major departures from the status quo (cf. Downs 1957). In a multi-dimensional space, however, there is no stable median. Instead, many possible combinations of policy packages can win majorities (Laver and Shepsle 1996; Strøm, Müller, and Bergman 2008). Parties can trade votes (log-roll) by offering their support in policy areas where they have less intense preferences in order to gain policy concessions in areas they assign high priority. If more dimensions are represented in the party system, this opens up the possibility for greater changes in policy. Whether this possibility bears fruit, however, depends on party interactions over time. In the Danish political system, it can be argued that the creation of the Danish People's Party in the 1990s brought a new political dimension into the party system. Today, the party combines an economic centre-left position with an extreme right position on value issues. It is best known for its intense anti-immigration stance, but also for its EU scepticism and generally anti-establishment positions. When the party was offered the role of permanent support party to the Liberal–Conservative party government of 2001–2011, this resulted in a series of new policies to tighten up on immigration. This was possible because economic policies were less important to the Danish Peoples' party than immigration (Christiansen and Pedersen 2014). Thus, negotiated agreements between political parties with partially different positions and emphasis enable new policy combinations and collaborative solutions to problems, despite internal differences.

Discussion of the model

So far we have laid out how political parties and innovation in public policy can be connected at the level of the party, its organization and policy programmes, as well as the party system and the policies represented. We assume throughout that politics and parties matter (cf. Schmidt 1996). Not all literature on parties supports this perspective, however. Some empirical studies show little or no impact of party government on major policy schemes such as public privatization (Helms 2016, 463). In an age of globalization, the role of political parties at national level is reduced. Theoretically, political parties could formulate policies in order to win elections (e.g. Downs 1957). In the latter conception, the origin of policy change lies in shifts in what voters want. In the former, parties may play a more active role in persuading voters of the merits of the policies they espouse. Naturally, there are theories that fall between the two perspectives and predict a mix between responsiveness and persuasiveness. Many would concur, however, that elections are blunt instruments when it comes to conveying information about preferences, and cannot provide parties with more than very vague guidelines. Even if parties only formulate policies to win office rather than the other way around, they still have a wide berth for selecting the exact policy instruments they will implement in office. The question is how this latitude is used.

Using our typology, we argue that the organizational links between civil society and political parties, as well as the intensity and richness of party programmes, are critical to whether parties matter. On the one hand, these linkages can be so tenuous that no real deliberation or negotiations take place within parties, and programmes can be little more than a collection of general aims and ideas if they exist at all. On the other hand, parties can be real political laboratories where input from different sources is discussed and entered in elaborate policy programmes. At the level of the party system, we argued that we need to look at patterns of government formation and alternation as well as the polarization of political positions and the number of salient policy dimensions in a system. Looking at these four aspects together enables us to formulate some general expectations.

At one extreme, we might expect the greatest potential for party-induced policy change and innovation in a government based on parties with strong organizational ties to civil society with richly developed programmes, where alternation has just occurred and the coalition consists of a new constellation of parties (or includes a new one), and where the parties represent different (but not polar opposite) positions and emphasize different policy dimensions. At the other extreme, we would expect to find governments based on a party with weak links to civil society, a vague and general political programme, a track record of having held office alone for a longer period (no alternation), and which represents views on a single political dimension. There are obviously many possible scenarios between the two extremes. We believe that it could be extremely fruitful to examine governments from this perspective and identify their characteristics based on properties taken from each of the four quadrants in the typology, which could then be related to their performance in the area of policy making. We propose that investigating whether parties matter requires an approach that takes their individual characteristics into account in concert with the conditions under which they operate.

Conclusion

Innovative policies are necessary to handle important twenty-first-century problems such as climate change, immigration and the development of the public sector to handle growing expectations from citizens. A sole focus on the role of bureaucratic actors in providing innovative solutions does not suffice. It is not only problematic for normative reasons, because it leaves out the democratically elected actors. It also limits a comprehensive understanding of the politics of innovation.

Our article has offered a framework to conceptualize innovation with regard to the role of political parties. It depends not just on what types of entity they are but also on the characteristics of the party systems they operate in from a formal or organizational point of view as well as from a substantial or policy perspective. While these aspects are never independent but always closely linked, we suggest that distinguishing between them brings clarity to analysis of these issues. We have argued that certain characteristics of parties and party systems – and particular combinations of these – are likely to be conducive to policy change and innovation, with the result that new goals or instruments are adopted (cf. Hall 1993). Other combinations of properties are likely to stifle departures from the status quo. In particular, we expect majoritarian two-party systems with parties that are highly centralized around a strong leadership to be better able to make decisions, which is usually a precondition for innovation. However, we also expect that sustainable and innovative ideas are more likely in multiparty consensus systems that involve stakeholders and display the will to find joint, collaborative solutions and overcome differences – these being an inevitable fact of life in politics – through negotiations.

The typology presented in this article is only a first step towards developing a theory of representational innovation. Further studies should develop testable hypotheses explaining when and why innovation will occur, and subject these theories to rigid empirical testing.

Disclosure statement

No potential conflict of interest was reported by the authors.

ORCID

Flemming Juul Christiansen http://orcid.org/0000-0002-3257-9323

References

Bale, T. 2003. "Cinderella and her Ugly Sisters: The Mainstream and Extreme right in Europe's Bipolarising Party Systems." *West European Politics* 26 (3): 67-90. doi:10.1080/01402380312331280598.

Bartolini, S. 1999. "Collusion, Competition and Democracy: Part I." *Journal of Theoretical Politics* 11 (4): 435-470. doi:10.1177/0951692899011004001.

Bartolini, S. 2000. "Collusion, Competition and Democracy: Part II." *Journal of Theoretical Politics* 12 (1): 33-65. doi:10.1177/0951692800012001002.

Bartolini, S., A. Chiaramonte, and R. D'Alimonte. 2004. "The Italian Party System between Parties and Coalitions." *West European Politics* 27 (1): 1-19. doi:10.1080/01402380412331280783.

Benoit, K. 2004. "Models of Electoral System Change." *Electoral Studies* 23 (3): 363-389. doi:10.1016/S0261-3794(03)00020-9.

Binder, S. 1999. "The Dynamics of Legislative Gridlock, 1947-96." *The American Political Science Review* 93 (3): 519-533. doi:10.2307/2585572.

Binder, S. 2015. "The Dysfunctional Congress." *Annual Review of Political Science* 18: 85-101. doi:10.1146/annurev-polisci-110813-032156.

Blondel, J. 1968. "Party Systems and Patterns of Government in Western Democracies." *Canadian Journal of Political Science* 1 (2): 180-203. doi:10.1017/S0008423900036507.

Christiansen, F. J., and E. Damgaard. 2008. "Parliamentary Opposition under Minority Parliamentarism: Scandinavia." *The Journal of Legislative Studies* 14 (1-2): 46-76. doi:10.1080/13572330801920937.

Christiansen, F. J., and H. H. Pedersen. 2014. "Minority Coalition Governance in Denmark." *Party Politics* 20 (6): 940-949. doi:10.1177/1354068812462924.

De Lange, S. 2007. "A New Winning Formula? The Programmatic Appeal of the Radical Right." *Party Politics* 13 (4): 411-435. doi:10.1177/1354068807075943.

De Vries, H., V. Bekkers, and L. Tummers. 2016. "Innovation in the Public Sector: A Systematic Review and Future Research Agenda." *Public Administration* 94 (1): 146-166. doi:10.1111/padm.2016.94.issue-1.

Downs, A. 1957. *An Economic Theory of Democracy*. New York: Harper & Row Publishers.

Duverger, M. 1954. *Political Parties: Their Organisation and Activity in the Modern State*. Methuen: Wiley.

Esping-Andersen, G. 1985. *Politics against Markets: The Social Democratic Road to Power*. Princeton, NJ: Princeton University Press.

Frankland, E. G., P. Lucardie, and B. Rihoux, eds. 2008. *Green Parties in Transition: The End of Grass-roots Democracy?* Farnham: Ashgate.

Green-Pedersen, C. 2004. "Center Parties, Party Competition, and the Implosion of Party Systems: A Study of Centripetal Tendencies in Multiparty Systems." *Political Studies* 52 (2): 324-341. doi:10.1111/j.1467-9248.2004.00482.x.

Green-Pedersen, C. 2007. "The Growing Importance of Issue Competition. The Changing Nature of Party Competition in Western Europe." *Political Studies* 55 (4): 608-628. doi:10.1111/j.1467-9248.2007.00686.x.

Hall, P. A. 1993. "Policy Paradigms, Social Learning, and the State: The Case of Economic Policymaking in Britain." *Comparative Politics* 25 3: 275-296. doi:10.2307/422246.

Harmel, R., and K. C. Janda. 1994. "An Integrated Theory of Party Goals and Party Change." *Journal of Theoretical Politics* 6 (3): 259-287. doi:10.1177/0951692894006003001.

Helms, L. 2016. "Democracy and Innovation: From Institutions to Agency and Leadership." *Democratization* 23 (3): 459-477. doi:10.1080/13510347.2014.981667.

Heywood, A. 2012. *Political Ideologies. An Introduction*. Basingstoke: Palgrave Macmillan.

Hooghe, L., and G. Marks. 2008. "European Union?" *West European Politics* 31 (1/2): 108-129. doi:10.1080/01402380701834739.

Hunt, B., and M. Laver. 1992. *Policy and Party Competition*. London: Routledge.

Katz, R. S., and P. Mair. 1995. "Changing Models of Party Organization and Party Democracy: The Emergence of the Cartel Party." *Party Politics* 1 (1): 5-28. doi:10.1177/1354068895001001001.

Kettl, D. F. 2002. *The Transformation of Governance*. Baltimore: The John Hopkins University Press.

Klingemann, H. D., A. Volkens, J. Bara, I. Budge, and M. D. McDonald. 2006. *Mapping Policy Preferences II. Comparing 24 OECD and 24 CEE Countries, 1990-2003*. Oxford: Oxford U.

Kooiman, J. 2003. *Governing as Governance*. London: Sage.
Krouwel, A. 2006. "Party Models." In *Handbook of Party Politics*, edited by R. S. Katz and W. J. Crotty, 249–269. London: Sage.
Laakso, M., and R. Taagepera. 1979. "The 'Effective' Number of Parties. A Measure with Application to West Europe." *Comparative Political Studies* 12 (1): 3–27.
Laver, M., and K. A. Shepsle. 1996. *Making and Breaking Governments: Cabinets and Legislatures in Parliamentary Democracies*. Cambridge: Cambridge University Press.
Lawson, K., and P. H. Merkl. 1988. *When Parties Fail. Emerging Alternative Organizations*. Princeton: Princeton University Press.
Lijphart, A. 1999. *Patterns of Democracy. Government Forms and Performance in Thirty-Six Countries*. New Haven: Yale University Press.
Lipset, S. M., and S. Rokkan. 1967. "Cleavage Structures, Party Systems, and Voter Alignments: An Introduction." In *Party Systems and Voter Alignment*, edited by S. M. Lipset and S. Rokkan, 1–64. New York: Free Press.
Mair, P. 2006. "Party System Change." In *Handbook of Party Politics*, edited by R. S. Katz and W. J. Crotty, 63–73. London: Sage.
Mair, P., and C. Mudde. 1998. "The Party Family and its Study." *Annual Review of Political Science* 1: 211–229. doi:10.1146/annurev.polisci.1.1.211.
Minstrom, M. 1997. "Policy Entrepreneurs and the Diffusion of Innovation." *American Journal of Political Science* 41 (3): 438–470.
Pitkin, H. 1967. *The Concept of Political Representation*. Berkeley: Los Angeles University Press.
Polsby, N. W. 1984. *Political Innovation in America: The Politics of Policy Innovation*. New Haven: Yale University Press.
Rogers, E. M. 2003. *Diffusion of Innovation*. 5th ed. New York: Free Press.
Røste, R. 2005. *Studies of Innovation in the Public Sector, a Theoretical Framework*. Publin Report D 16. Oslo: Nifu Step.
Sartori, G. 1976. *Party and Party Systems. A Framework for Analysis*. Vol. I. Cambridge: Cambridge University Press.
Schmidt, M. G. 1996. "When Parties Matter: A Review of the Possibilities and Limits of Partisan Influence on Public Policy." *European Journal of Political Research* 30 (2): 155–183. doi:10.1111/ejpr.1996.30.issue-2.
Schumpeter, J. 1934. *The Theory of Economic Development*. Cambridge, MA: Harvard University Press.
Sørensen, E. 2016. "Political Innovations: Innovations in Political Institutions, Processes and Outputs." *Public Management Review*. doi:10.1080/14719037.2016.1200661.
Sørensen, E., and J. Torfing. 2011. "Enhancing Collaboration in the Public Sector." *Administration and Society* 43 (8): 842–868. doi:10.1177/0095399711418768.
Strøm, K., W. C. Müller, and T. Bergman. 2008. *Cabinets and Coalition Bargaining: The Democratic Life Cycle in Western Europe*. Oxford: Oxford University Press.
Tsebelis, G. 2002. *Veto Players: How Political Institutions Work*. Princeton: Princeton University Press.
Van der Brug, W., and A. Mughan. 2007. "Charisma, Leader Effects, and Support for Right-Wing Populist Parties." *Party Politics* 13 (1): 29–51. doi:10.1177/1354068806071260.
Vassallo, F., and C. Wilcox. 2006. "Party as Carrier of Ideas." In *Handbook of Party Politics*, edited by R. S. Katz and W. J. Crotty, 413–421. London: Sage.
Voorberg, W., V. J. J. M. Bekkers, and L. G. Tummers. 2015. "A Systematic Review of Co-Creation and Co-Production: Embarking on the Social Innovation Journey." *Public Management Review* 17 (9): 1333–1357. doi:10.1080/14719037.2014.930505.
Warwick, P. V. 2002. "Toward a Common Dimensionality in West European Policy Spaces." *Party Politics* 8 (1): 101–122. doi:10.1177/1354068802008001005.
Webb, P., T. Poguntke, and R. Kolodny. 2012. "The Presidentialization of Party Leadership? Evaluating Party Leadership and Party Government in the Democratic World." In *Comparative Political Leadership*, edited by L. Helms, 77–98. Basingstoke: Palgrave Macmillan.
Zons, G. 2015. "The Influence of Programmatic Diversity on the Formation of New Political Parties." *Party Politics* 21 (6): 919–929. doi:10.1177/1354068813509515.

Assessing the impact of informal governance on political innovation

Sarah Ayres

ABSTRACT
The aim of this article is to examine the role played by 'informal governance' in shaping political innovation. Informal governance can be defined as a means of decision-making that is un-codified, non-institutional and where social relationships play crucial roles. This article explores the impact of informal governance on three dimensions of political innovation – innovations in polity (institutions), politics (process) and policy (outcomes). It argues that an analysis of informal governance is essential if we are to fully understand how political innovation occurs. Research evidence suggests that even when formal structures and procedures are weak political innovation can still thrive.

Introduction

This article examines the role of 'informal governance' in shaping political innovation. In the introduction to this Special Issue, particular attention is given to innovations in political institutions, processes and outcomes – or what Sørensen (2016) refers to as 'polity, politics and policy'. This way of conceptualizing public innovation takes account of the political context in which governments seek to promote innovation and change. These three dimensions will be used to frame an analysis of how informal governance shapes political innovation in distinct ways. Informal governance can be defined 'as a means of decision-making that is un-codified, non-institutional and where social relationships and webs of influence play crucial roles' (Harsh 2013, 481). It can shape political innovation in both positive and negative ways. On the one hand, informal governance can assist in solving political and policy problems which cannot easily be solved by traditional government institutions, leading to more effective and innovative decision-making. On the other, it may weaken transparency, accountability and legitimacy by undermining traditional (more formal) administrative structures (Lauth 2013).

The issue of informality in policymaking is particularly timely as public managers seek to manage multifaceted policy problems within contested and uncertain environments. Political decision-making has increasing moved away from the national level of government to a more spatially diverse, temporal and fluid set of arrangements (Jessop 2016). Hajer (2003) refers to policymaking increasingly taking place in an 'institutional void where there is no generally accepted rules and norms according to which politics is to be conducted'. Others argue that it is the surge of 'wicked problems' that have prompted this type of leadership as multiple actors come together to solve policy problems (Klijn and Koppenjan 2016). Finally, in many countries the recent global financial crisis has resulted in a reduction in state capacity that has prompted a new style of political leadership – one that relies less on bureaucracy and more on informal relations.

These developments raise important questions about how informal governance operates in this transforming policy landscape and the impact it has on political innovation. There is comparatively little research on the role of informality in policymaking, partly because of the complexity of studying it (van Jitske and van Buuren 2015). This article responds to this gap by placing informal governance at its heart. The role played by informal governance in shaping political innovation will be examined through a case study of English devolution in the UK. This area of policy is highly suited to analyse informal governance for the following reasons. First, the current Conservative government is committed to extensive devolution of power to local government. Yet, there is very little formal guidance shaping the scope and direction of the policy (Political Studies Association 2016). Second, informality is pertinent to the current devolution debate as the government is proposing a range of 'devolution deals' with localities, each of which is to be individually brokered – a combination in reality of formal 'front stage' politics and informal 'back stage' negotiations (Klijn 2014). Third, there is a high degree of complexity and uncertainty evident and the focus on negotiation means that informal governance is more likely to feature (Klijn and Koppenjan 2016). These features are characteristic of Hajer's (2003) concept of 'policy without polity' – where policymaking is increasingly occurring in an institutional void. This case study provides an opportunity to explore how informal governance influences policymaking in an institutional void and the implications this has for political innovation.

The analysis is from a central government perspective and focuses on three distinct levels. First, changes in the institutional arrangements that regulate and authorize policymaking will be explored. These are referred to as *innovations in polity*, defined as

> intentional efforts to reorganize the external boundaries to other polities as well as the institutional framework and procedures that regulate the formation and enactment of democratically authorized decisions. (Sørensen 2016)

Crucial to this dimension is the complex interplay between formal institutional arrangements and more informal practices. Second, it will explore the impact of informal governance on the processes involved in negotiating the current round of devolution deals. These processes are referred to as *innovations in politics*. Sørensen (2016) defines innovations in politics as 'the development and realization of new ways for political actors to obtain democratically legitimate political power and influence'. Central to this analysis is the role played by critical actors, or boundary spanners, in the process (Guarneros-Meza and Martin 2014). Third, *innovations in policy* involve the 'formulation and elaboration of new political visions, goals, strategies, and policy programmes' (2014). This section will examine the role of informality in shaping new political visions and strategies amongst senior Whitehall officials charged with managing English devolution.

This article is structured as follows. The next section provides a brief description of the policy context. This is followed by the theoretical framework, which includes how the concepts of political innovation and informal governance have been operationalized. The research methodology and data analysis and findings sections follow. Research findings are presented in three parts that examine the impact of informal governance on innovations in polity, politics and policy. The article concludes by reflecting on how insights from this case study might be utilized in a broader context – theoretically, methodologically and in practice.

Policy background: devolution and the governance of England

The UK is one of the most centralized countries of its size in the developed world and 'English local government has the most circumscribed powers of any equivalent tier internationally' (Institute for Government 2014, 3). Decentralization has the potential to boost economic growth, allow for variation and innovation in public services and enhance local democracy. All the main UK political parties recognize this possibility and have been good at making commitments to devolve power. Nonetheless, successive governments have found it hard to implement decentralizing reforms due to a complex set of cultural and institutional barriers.

Elected in May 2015, the current Conservative government set out ambitious plans in its Manifesto 'to devolve powers and budgets to boost local growth in England' (Conservative Party 2015, 1). That same document pledged to devolve 'far-reaching powers over economic development, transport and social care to large cities which choose to have elected mayors' (2015, 1). The government was swift to implement the Cities and Local Government Devolution Bill (Department for Communities and Local Government (DCLG) & the Home Office 2015) to make good this pledge. This bill is an enabling piece of legislation allowing the government to proceed on a case-by-case basis to reach a tailor-made deal with each participating locality (Localis and Grant Thornton 2015). A high degree of variability is anticipated both in terms of the *process* of negotiating the deal and the final policy *outcome*. Some commentators have expressed concern about spatial and social justice given that individual areas will benefit differentially from this process (Smith and Richards 2015). Others have criticized the lack of transparency in the way that the new deals have been brokered (Centre for Public Scrutiny 2015). Despite this, there is a strong political drive for devolution. The current challenge for policymakers and administrators is to achieve political innovation where previous governments have failed.

To date, 11 devolution deals have been negotiated between central government and local areas. Sandford (2016, 18) describes the devolution deals as

> consisting of a menu with specials. A number of items have been made available to most areas, but each deal also contains a few unique elements or specials.

Many of the deals so far cover areas such as further education, business support, unemployment services, EU Structural Funds, fiscal powers, integrated transport plans, local planning and land use. However, there is differentiation. For example, because of its history of productive local partnership working, the Greater Manchester Combined Authority is viewed by government as the model of best practice regards the deals. It has, therefore, been granted control over policy areas not previously devolved in England, including the ability to integrate health, social care and children's services (for a comprehensive account, see Sandford 2016).

The government set a deadline of 4 September 2015 for submissions to be considered and a total of 38 bids were submitted (Department for Communities and Local Government (DCLG) & the Home Office 2015). The data presented in this article focuses on the *process* of negotiating these deals between senior Whitehall officials and local actors. It will not discuss the details of individual localities or specific deals as this could jeopardize confidentiality agreements. Instead, this article will identify patterns of responses in the beliefs, perceptions and behaviours of senior Whitehall officials engaged in negotiating devolution deals. These insights will provide thick, rich descriptions of the day-to-day working practices of those involved to allow an examination of how they perceive and use informal governance to shape political innovations.

Literature review: political innovation and informal governance

Political innovation and informal governance

Innovation, as distinct from invention, refers to the adoption of something new to its adopters (Rogers 2003). Public-sector innovation can be defined as 'the adoption, creation or development of ideas, objects and practices that are new to the unit of adoption' (Jiannan, Liang, and Yuqian 2013, 350). This definition encompasses a broad range of activities, including the construction, communication and implementation of new ideas and practices. Indeed, there are a range of interpretations offered by scholars on the typologies, dimensions and characteristics of public innovation (Osborne and Brown 2013). While many of these dimensions are pertinent, this article examines the role of informal governance in shaping political innovation across the three dimensions relevant to this Special Issue: polity, politics and policy.

The distinction between 'front stage' and 'back stage' policymaking is drawn upon. Friedman (1995, 16) suggests that 'front stage, actors are visible to the audience and have to stay in role'. Public officials are visible and accountable as office holders to elected bodies and are constrained by established bureaucratic rules, codes of conduct and public scrutiny (Klijn 2014). Back stage describes the world of complex decision-making where public officials are hidden from public scrutiny and can engage in complex negotiations less constrained by formal rules. 'Back stage, actors can relax from their roles, step out of character and work with their dramaturgical teammates to prepare for the front stage performance' (Friedman 1995, 17). Back stage, informal governance may thrive and this flexibility can enhance innovative capacity. Indeed, Torfing et al. (2012) argue that a degree of 'seclusion' is often necessary in order to govern effectively. The potential advantages of informal governance for each of the three dimensions of political innovation – polity, politics and policy – are set out below.

Innovations in polity: examining the institutions

Innovations in polity refers to the formal and informal institutional processes and practices in place to organize policymaking (Sørensen 2016). Formal structures are regulated by rules that have been instituted according to procedures recognized as legal in clearly defined contexts. By contrast, 'informal practices refer to interactions that occur in formal contexts, but according to mechanisms which are effective in wider everyday life' (Brie and Stolting 2013, 19). Informal (back stage) practices can offer a number of benefits for innovations in polity. This includes creating an innovative space for 'inspiring, nurturing, supporting and communicating' (Kickert, Klijn, and Koppenjan 1997, 11), activating (and deactivating) critical actors and resources, promoting streamlined structures (Torfing et al. 2012) and developing trust. Trust is a valuable asset in the promotion of political innovation. It can tackle strategic uncertainty and enhance the possibility of actors sharing information and developing innovative solutions (Lane and Bachman 1998). To work effectively, however, informal practices must complement the formal. Friedman (1995, 17) notes that a key challenge is for actors to 'construct a back stage environment as well as front stage drama, and to manage the movement between these stages'. Nonetheless, this might be especially difficult in an 'institutional void' (Hajer 2003), where new formal rules and models of legitimacy are being re-negotiated in fluid spaces.

Innovations in politics: examining the process

Innovations in politics will be examined by exploring how senior Whitehall officials are utilizing informal governance to navigate their working environment. Organizational culture is pivotal in shaping the parameters within which public managers can pursue informal and innovative practices and think creatively about their roles. An 'innovative-oriented culture encompasses both the intention to be innovative and the creation of a supportive climate for innovation' (Wynen et al. 2014, 46). Political leaders must grant administrators with sufficient autonomy and flexibility to promote innovation-oriented behaviour. However, this can be challenging in public bureaucracies which have a disposition to reduce uncertainty and pursue stability (Hartley, Sørensen, and Torfing 2013). Operating back stage can, however, help to overcome the predisposition for bureaucratic conservatism. It can empower administrators, or boundary spanners (Guarneros-Meza and Martin 2014), by encouraging them to use their full professional discretion. This can lead to a dynamic culture of entrepreneurship. Operating back stage provides an opportunity to deploy 'soft power' (Newman 2012) to exert influence. However, elected politicians and public managers may still be held to account for their decisions back stage rendering some measure of transparency and accountability necessary (Ferreira da Cruz et al. 2015). To ensure this, Reh (2013) suggests that informal governance needs a 'formalization' phase. Informal practices must re-engage with formal structures for informal policy visions, goals and strategies to be ratified, codified and for them to have traction and legitimacy.

Innovations in policy: examining the outcomes

Innovations in policy are 'deliberate efforts to develop and promote new political visions, goals, strategies and policy programmes' (Sørensen 2016). Polsby (1984) highlights the tension between the political and administrative aspects of policy innovation. Politicians have an important front-stage role in developing a narrative and building public support for innovation before it occurs and mobilizing various stakeholders. Crucially, they can 'provide the right climate to enable managers and staff to experiment, and they can challenge technical thinking, combining it with political astuteness' (Hartley 2014, 231). By contrast, public managers are responsible for turning political aspirations into policy reality. Informal (back stage) governance offers a number of distinct advantages in overcoming the barriers to policy innovation. It can help to clarify shared goals, provide an opportunity to seek novel and responsive policy solutions and create the commitment required for long-term policy success (Klijn 2014).

The use of informal governance does, however, raise important questions about accountability and democracy in policy innovation. Fung (2012) argues that policy innovation needs to be mindful of the pursuit of democratic ideals and improvements. However, Borzel and Panke (2012) argue that concerns about transparency and legitimacy in policymaking are often neglected behind the pursuit of effectiveness. Based on this review of the literature, three propositions have been developed to examine the role of informal governance in shaping political innovation:

- Innovations in polity: Informal governance creates an 'innovative space' to explore new possibilities and develop trust between critical actors.
- Innovations in politics: Informal governance can be used to enhance the autonomy and discretion of administrators, leading to an 'innovative oriented culture'.
- Innovations in policy: Informal governance can lead to more responsive problem solving and a shared commitment to new policy goals.

Each of these propositions will be explored in the data analysis section below.

Operationalizing informal governance

Formal and informal governance is evident in all political systems and may complement, support, impede or paralyse each other. A key challenge is to distinguish what is 'informal' or just part of the bureaucratic process of public administration. Clarifying this distinction is central to operationalizing this research. Most work exploring informal governance has focused on the supranational level in an attempt to capture the complexity and fluidity of policymaking in multilevel and multiactor settings (Christiansen and Neuhold 2013). This article draws on and develops a framework adopted by Van Tatenhove, Mak, and Liefferink (2006) who identify (i) a working definition of informal governance, (ii) the strategic motives behind informal practices and (iii) the arenas where informal governance takes place. Although originally conceived as a tool to examine European policymaking, this approach is deemed suitable to explore the impact of informal governance on political innovation as it deals with the complex interplay between formal and informal arrangements.

(i) *The definition*: Van Tatenhove, Mak, and Liefferink (2006, 14) define informal governance as

> those non-codified settings of day-to-day interaction concerning policy issues, in which the participation of actors, the formation of coalitions, the processes of agenda setting, (preliminary) decision-making and implementation are not structured by pre-given sets of rules or formal institutions.

Two concepts are central. First, whether settings are codified or formally sanctioned by legitimate actors. Formal sanctioning can be derived from

Table 1. Origins of formal sanctioning and rules of the game.

Forms of governance	Formal sanctioning	Rules of the game
Hierarchy	Bureaucracy	Government statute, guidance, strategies
Markets	Contracts	Contractual agreements, legal documents
Networks	Collaboration	Partnership agreements, protocols

Source: Author's own.

hierarchy, market and networked forms of governance. It refers to the question of whether practices are based on a *script* agreed and recognized by legitimate actors. Second are the 'rules of the game' and the way that rules guide and constrain the behaviour of actors (Table 1).

(ii) *The motives*: Informal practices can be accidental, pragmatic, intentional, interest-driven or ideological. Van Tatenhove *et al.* suggest that the specific interplay of informal and formal practices depends on the strategic intent of the actors involved. They distinguish between two strategic motives: cooperative strategies focus on *facilitating* the formal policy process. Informal practices then play the role of an *innovative space* for new rules, which may become formalized at a later stage. In conflicting strategies, actors are motivated by a desire to change formal practices by, for example, raising their *critical voice* in objection to policy or deliberately try to *subvert* formal rules (Table 2). This framework has been employed to analyse whether Whitehall officials were using informal governance to facilitate or undermine the formal political objectives of elected politicians.

(iii) *The arenas*: A distinction is made between *front stage* and *back stage*. 'Front stage' is the place where roles are performed before an audience, i.e. where actors from state, market and civil society come together in formal settings based on codified rules of the game. In 'back stage', the roles of actors or rules of the game are not given beforehand. Back stage is concerned with rule altering arrangements that evolve on the ground in the interactions between actors. Eventually, practices developed back stage may trickle down to the front stage as codified rules. Table 3 emphasizes the relationship between the strategic motives behind informal governance and the arenas where governance takes place. The vertical axis addresses whether practices are taking place front stage (pregiven rules) or back stage (no pregiven rules). The

Table 2. Motives behind the emergence of informal practices.

Strategies	Cooperative	Conflicting
Rule-directed (pregiven rules)	Facilitating	Critical voice
Rule-altering (no pregiven rules)	Innovative space	Subversive

Source: Author's own, adapted from Van Tatenhove, Mak, and Liefferink (2006, 15).

Table 3. Formal and informal governance arenas.

Arenas	Formally sanctioned	Not formally sanctioned
Front stage (rule-directed, pregiven rules)	1. Formal front stage	2. Informal front stage *Facilitating* *Critical voice*
Back stage (rule-altering, no pregiven rules)	3. Formally sanctioned backstage *Innovative space*	4. Sub-politics *Subversive*

Source: Author's own, adapted from Van Tatenhove, Mak, and Liefferink (2006, 17).

horizontal axis deals with questions of whether the settings are codified or formally sanctioned on not. Only cell 1 represents a classical type of formal governance, based on formally sanctioned and codified rules and procedures. Cells 2–4 represent different kinds of informal governance because they are either not formally sanctioned and/or there are no pregiven rules. Not formally sanction means that there is no pre-agreed script or set of procedures to guide interactions, rather than actors disobeying a script. This framework has been utilized to make the distinction between formal and informal governance in the empirical analysis.

Research methods

This study adopts an in-depth qualitative methodology aimed at providing so-called 'thick descriptions' of the day-to-day practices guiding political actions (Rhodes 2013). The empirical work is based on 22 in-depth, semi-structured interviews conducted between September and December 2015 with senior Whitehall officials charged with negotiating devolution deals between central government and local areas. Respondents were identified through established professional contacts, a search of departmental websites and snowballing. Interviews were conducted with officials working in the Treasury, Cabinet Office and the Departments for Business, Innovation and Skills (BIS); Communities and Local Government (DCLG) and Transport (DfT). Respondents were asked a series of questions about formal and informal procedures for negotiating devolution deals. These included, whether they recognized the use of informality in the process, their motivations for using informal governance, their perceptions on the advantages and disadvantages of informal working and the impact of informal governance on the policy process. Interviews were conducted under 'Chatham House Rules' and lasted between 60 and 90 min. They were digitally recorded, professionally transcribed and manually coded to elicit findings.

Respondents were remarkably frank and able to recognize and articulate examples of informal governance. Nonetheless, three caveats are worth noting. First, interviewees represented individuals at the heart of devolution negotiations. Their insider status afforded them influence that is unlikely to be shared by a more diverse range of stakeholders. Therefore, their motivation and use of informal governance may not be emblematic of the broader policy network. Second, devolution in England is high on the government's agenda and is operating under the close guardianship of high-profile ministers. Therefore, the political momentum and the pace of political innovation in this area are not necessarily characteristic of UK policymaking in general. Third, the devolution agenda is characterized by a high degree of informal governance – typical of Hajer's (2003) 'institutional void'. This provides an interesting opportunity to explore the impact of informal governance on political innovation in a policy environment where regulation is relatively weak.

Data analysis and findings

Innovations in polity: examining the institutions

Institutional processes and practices for developing devolution deals have been described as 'almost entirely secret' with details 'being released only when agreements have been reached' (Centre for Public Scrutiny 2015, 8). However, formal procedures do exist. Interviewees suggested that negotiations for devolution deals were directed by a series of formally sanctioned rules, not least the government's manifesto, Devolution Bill and ministerial speeches. Indeed, a number front-stage institutional arrangements were identified which guided interactions and 'formalized' informal working at critical points (Reh 2013). This included a cross-departmental team (Cities and Local Growth Team) to oversee the deals. Respondents also referred to the use of emails to provide a formal mechanism to record agreements and conversations,

> Civil servants learn to make sure that we record things we think might be useful to record for posterity. But, we want to be careful about getting the right balance between doing that to legitimately cover your back versus just recoding everything to the extent that it becomes unfeasible. (HM Treasury official)

Written drafts of the devolution bids were also circulated at critical points, and when more formal meetings did occur, for example between local leaders and ministers, these would be minuted and formally archived. Devolution deals were formally signed off via Whitehall's Cabinet Committee procedures and local areas had their own procedures. Finally, the deals were signed in public by the minister and local leaders.

All respondents agreed, however, that central–local relations were increasingly based on informal governance as compared with arrangements under previous governments. Officials agreed that the main drive had come from a clear steer from ministers and the contents of the Devolution Bill, which was broadly acknowledged to be purposefully low on guidance (Department for Communities and Local Government (DCLG) & the Home Office 2015). In their view, 'the Minister for Communities and Local Government had expressed a clear preference for process light arrangements' (HM Treasury official). A DCLG official illustrated this point,

> The Minister [Secretary of State for Communities and Local Government] personally believes very strongly in negotiation. His presence in this agenda, in terms of ministerial continuity and leadership, is extremely important. There is a clear Ministerial ambition on bespoke deals that drives informal working. We have a set of Ministers, including the Chancellor, who are very much more comfortable without the need for a 50 page guidance document. So, this green light from the top builds insurances through the bureaucracy to be able to work more loosely.

Whitehall officials were overwhelmingly motivated to use informal governance to pursue *cooperative* strategies to either *facilitate* the formal process or creative an *innovative space* to explore new possibilities. Many agreed that using informal governance, to facilitate the formal bureaucracy when necessary, was often the best way to achieve policy objectives – essentially managing the complex interplay between front and back stage (Friedman 1995). Most suggested that informal working had enhanced the effectiveness of the, albeit limited, formal institutional arrangements. For example, interpersonal relationships were used to create an 'innovative space' to bring reluctant actors into discussions. A number of interviewees referred to building 'trust' as essential in creating a polity conducive to exploring public innovation (Klijn, Steijn, and Edelenbos 2010), as an HM Treasury official suggested,

> What my team have been able to do is really develop and broker very informal relationships and trust. The leader of [local] Council called me yesterday. He wanted some informal advice.

He knew that he could trust me and that I would tell him the best way to pitch his point to colleagues in the civil service and Ministers. He couldn't have done that formally so I see my role as bringing them together.

In this way, officials were essentially able to (re)configure the policy network (Klijn and Koppenjan 2016) in subtle ways by activating critical actors and resources. Interviewees overwhelmingly viewed this as an effective means to move the devolution agenda forward. This was particularly important given the political pressure to secure a number of high-profile deals in a short period of time. As a DCLG official commented, 'if negotiations were held in public and open to full scrutiny we wouldn't have got off first base'. Officials were, however, mindful of the potential challenges of translating high trust between individuals at an institutional level. This was made all the more challenging by the significant amount of movement in the Whitehall civil service. Some respondents sought to mitigate these risks by 'managing the handover effectively and fully briefing new colleagues on the softer, more relational aspects' (HM Treasury official). Others suggested that the turnover of staff was 'also a problem when operating through more formal bureaucratic structures so informal governance posed no greater risk' (DCLG official).

A number of respondents were motivated to use informal governance to pursue *conflicting* strategies but, crucially, not to undermine the government's objectives. Instead, conflicting strategies were motivated by a desire to change the polities or practices of local actors with whom they were negotiating. For example, this might involve informal advice on central government's preferred local people to work with or how to improve the content of local plans. In this way, informal governance had a significant role in reorganizing the external boundaries of Whitehall to other local polities (Sørensen 2016). Finally, there was very little evidence of officials being motivated to use informal governance to *subvert* formal arrangements. This might be explained by the high degree political consensus between elected leaders and senior bureaucrats combined with the fact that the agenda was taking place in an 'institutional void' (Hajer 2003), where there were actually very few rules to subvert (Department for Communities and Local Government (DCLG) & the Home Office 2015). Table 4 summarizes evidence of informal governance, the innovations in polity and potential pitfalls to more informal ways of working.

Innovations in politics: examining the process

Elected politicians had provided a clear narrative to empower public managers to use informal working. This proved critical in providing an 'innovative-oriented culture'

Table 4. The impact of informal governance on innovations in polity.

Manifestations of informal working	Innovation in polity	Potential pitfalls
Process light arrangements and limited policy guidance	Creation of an 'innovative space'	Translating personal trust into institutional trust
Political sanctioning of informal procedures	(Re) configuration of network actors and assets	Elitist decision-making and potential exclusion of interested parties
Few rules and lack of an agreed script to manage intergovernmental relationships	Harnessing trust as a collaborative asset	
	Strong political momentum	

(Wynen et al. 2014). Officials felt that a strong mandate from elected politicians engendered a degree of legitimacy and accountability in their use of informality (Hartley 2014). It is, however, also possible that this emerging central government narrative of dynamism, autonomy and invention could be interpreted as a conveniently constructed script to mask the underlying pressures of public-sector cuts and 'needs must' arrangements that would be far less palatable as a public discourse. Although not a view expressed by interviewees, one might ascribe the transition to greater informality as bordering on the chaotic and the antithesis of good governance (Smith and Richards 2015). Although beyond the scope of this analysis, it would be interesting to ascertain how stakeholders outside central government viewed this transition.

What appears to have emerged in Whitehall is a group of highly skilled administrative boundary spanners, linked by an increasingly dense and more frequent layer of informal relationships. These individuals were able to 'facilitate partnership working by acting as informational facilitators and, by virtue of their nodal position and interpersonal skills, resolve inter-organizational conflicts and build mutual understanding and trust among partners' (Guarneros-Meza and Martin 2014, 2). They were involved in high-level negotiations and had senior positions within their respective departments, making them ideally placed to use soft power (Newman 2012),

> There is genuinely no script and this is why the responsibility lies with more senior officials. Using informal mechanisms is in the nature of our jobs. You have to be a skilled administrator with enough seniority to make strategic decisions. In drawing on these skills we are creating a space and a set of conditions where the right strategic decisions can be taken. (DCLG official)

The opportunity for informality was particularly evident in negotiations *prior* to the formal submissions of the deals in September 2015. Whitehall officials were utilizing an innovative-oriented culture to think creatively about new ways to secure power and influence. These innovative processes were increasingly happening 'below the radar of the formal bureaucratic structures' (HM Treasury official) often without a clearly defined audit trail. There was also a view that some of the tough and frank discussions required to strike deals would be extremely difficult to have on the record and informal governance provided a safe space 'where we wouldn't want the public or our colleagues monitoring our every conversation' (DCLG official). Here informality was often used to overcome political or institutional barriers and to break deadlocks (Hartley, Sørensen, and Torfing 2013). Whitehall officials felt that informal working had been largely positive, an observation supported by Localis and Grant Thornton (2015, 16) who suggested that '72% of local actors had found the discussions with central government constructive and positive'. For example, getting local areas to reach an agreement on the imposition of a metro mayor was an area Whitehall officials repeatedly referred to as requiring soft power.

> The introduction of a metro mayor was turning into a deal breaker in [locality]. In the end we invited local leaders to Whitehall for an informal discussion. There were only six of us in the room and both sides lay their cards on the table. It was the only way an agreement like that could have been secured. (DCLG official)

The potential risks associated with informality were, however, acknowledged including the resource-intensive nature of relationships building, the danger of mixed messages and a lack of transparency (Helmke and Levitsky 2013). A small number of respondents expressed some of the need to provide an adequate audit trail for decision-making. Officials looked to overcome these pitfalls by 'formalizing' informal activities at critical points (Reh 2013),

> We did go through as rigorous process as we could to make sure that we had some kind of moderation to make sure there was consistency, albeit in a limited way. We have to have a defensible audit trail if someone wants to come in at a later stage to evaluate this process but it was light touch. (BIS official)

Nonetheless, one official, who did not want their views to be ascribed to their department, outlined the potential risk of informal working with local partners,

> It [using informal governance] hasn't come a cropper yet. But, the one thing that there hasn't been but there is perhaps a fear of is a local leader getting to the point where they just say in public 'we are going to expose this for the sham that it is' or something like that. Now, that would be unfair but those kind of accusations might derail this process.

Smith and Richards (2015, 22) suggest that there has been a lack of clarity over the process for agreeing deals, with Whitehall devolving powers according to unwritten rules, which 'has the potential to create a patchwork system of devolution based on Whitehall concessions and not democratic rights'. A key question will be whether managing devolution deals in this way, back stage, will undermine implementation in the future when consensus and compliance from a broader range of stakeholders will be required. Table 5 summarizes evidence of informal governance, innovations in politics and the potential pitfalls of more informal working.

Innovations in policy: examining the outcomes

The use of informal governance identified in this article raises some important questions about the tension between political and administrative drives for policy innovation. First, elected politicians have been pivotal in shaping this agenda, top-down, through strong ministerial leadership that has stimulated confidence amongst officials throughout the bureaucracy. The evidence presented here supports the view that a productive relationship between policymakers and administrators is beneficial in securing policy innovation (Hartley, Sørensen, and Torfing 2013). Political leaders were pivotal in setting the agenda, while public managers assumed the role of policy innovators (Polsby 1984). In contrast to arguments of 'depoliticization' (Flinders and Wood 2014), the evidence presented here indicates a strong political mandate that is engendered throughout the bureaucracy and downwards through multiple levels of governance (Aucoin 2012).

Table 5. The impact of informal governance on innovations in politics.

Manifestations of informal working	Innovation in politics	Potential pitfalls
New ministerial narrative in support of informal working	Creation of an 'innovative-oriented culture'	Informal relationships and processes are resource intensive
Empowerment of senior administrators to go 'off script' and utilize informal working	Emergence of a group of highly skilled boundary spanners	Danger of mixed messages in negotiations
	Breaking deadlocks in difficult negotiations	
Pursuit of new and creative informal ways to seek power and influence	New processes to 'formalize' informal decision-making at critical points	Lack of transparency and audit in decision- making

The institutional arrangements and processes described above have served to develop and promote new political visions, goals and strategies in the area of UK devolution policy (Jiannan, Liang, and Yuqian 2013). First, evidence suggests that a clear ministerial narrative combined with the facilitating strategies of senior officials have produced a new vision in Whitehall regards the management of central–local relations. A DCLG official suggested that

> We used to micromanage local government and give them clear instructions and templates to follow. Now the emphasis is far more on locally-led, bottom-up solutions and local areas doing their own problem solving with our support. That has been a significant change for central government with its historical tendency to impose control through established procedures.

Whitehall officials were utilizing high trust relationships with local actors to influence policy outcomes. For example, when one respondent failed to influence the views of a minister via the formal bureaucracy they asked a number of local leaders to make the same appeal to the minister in a signed letter, which the Whitehall official drafted. The official's involvement in this process was not disclosed to the minister and the letter had the desired effect. Formally, it was the letter from local leaders that resulted in a change of position. However, an analysis of informal governance revealed that it was the 'back stage' positioning and influence of this Whitehall official, working in conjunction with their local partners that secured the policy innovation. This is evidence of *subversive* behaviour. However, the official asserted that it was an attempt to utilize informal governance to change policy outcomes 'by side stepping formal procedures for good intent'. While this example, and others, represents non-sanctioned, rule-altering behaviours, motivated by conflicting strategies, they were ultimately about trying to progress the agenda in positive ways. In all cases of *subversion*, the motive of officials was to bypass elements of formal governance deemed inefficient. These findings confirm Borzel and Panke's (2012) view that often a degree of 'due process' and transparency is sacrificed to promote greater effectiveness.

Second, evidence also pointed to a new vision of what might be described as 'unashamed diversity' both in the way that Whitehall officials were engaging local actors and also in the final policy outcomes. The inevitability of local winners and losers appeared to be a position that Whitehall officials 'were increasingly more comfortable with' (HM Treasury official). Whitehall officials regarded the bespoke deals as far 'more responsive to local circumstances' (BIS official). However, the pace with which the agenda has unfolded has placed a huge strain on central government resources. Territorial equity and spatial justice could be threatened by a lack of Whitehall capacity to invest in the high-intensity relationships required to secure bespoke deals in all English localities.

Third, the development of high trust central–local relationships resulted in new policy areas being devolved in some localities. The Department of Health, for example, has traditionally been one of the most resistant to devolution (Ayres and Pearce 2013). However, securing the integration of health and social care as one of the 'specials' (Sandford 2016) in 'the Manchester Combined Authority deal signals what can be achieved when shared goals are created and assurances of competence are secured' (HM Treasury official).

Table 6. The impact of informal governance on innovations in policy.

Manifestations of informal working	Innovation in policy	Potential pitfalls
Political leaders and managers working informally to reach shared goals	New vision for managing central–local relations	Administrators being politicized by the process
Focus on long-term relationship building with localities	Increased diversity in central–local relationships and policy outcomes	A lack of capacity could undermine equity and fairness in the process
Focus on negotiation and bespoke deals	New policy areas (e.g. health) to be devolved	Central power is enforced informally, undermining local discretion

Commentators are currently divided, however, on whether these changes epitomize a new political commitment in Whitehall to devolve power where previous governments have failed or whether the agenda represents a 'devolution deception', whereby government presents a façade of devolution while maintaining ultimate control (Hambleton 2015). Evidence of the use of informal governance supports both these positions. While all respondents indicated that they were utilizing informal governance with a 'view to devolving as much as possible' (DCLG official) it was also clear that central government was clearly in control of what, where and how devolution should occur. By using informal means to shape local aspirations behind closed doors, the 'shadow of hierarchy' was operationalized in more subtle ways, thus potentially supporting claims of a devolution deception. In this argument, by the time the deals were submitted and in the public domain, Whitehall's imposition of policy preferences would remain largely masked. Table 6 summarizes evidence of informal governance, the innovations in policy and potential pitfalls.

Conclusions

Research evidence suggests that informal governance played a significant role in shaping all three dimensions of political innovation in the area of English devolution policy. Indeed, this might have been assumed already. However, this article makes a distinct contribution to the field of public innovation by providing empirically grounded evidence to scientifically support this assertion. The evidence presented here makes a contribution to an area, acknowledged to be highly influential in shaping political innovation, but where there has been a lack of empirical work (van Jitske and van Buuren 2015). The case study is emblematic of policymaking in an 'institutional void' (Hajer 2003), whereby formal regulation was relatively weak. This has afforded an opportunity for informal governance to determine political innovation in distinct ways. More formal arenas are arguably less likely to utilize informal governance in this way. Yet, this need not equate with less political innovation in formal settings. Instead, other critical resources, such as leadership or bureaucracy, might be drawn upon to pursue political innovation. What this research evidence tells us is that when formal structures and procedures are weak, political innovation can still thrive. Indeed, operating 'back stage' offers a number of distinct advantages for political innovation (Klijn 2014), although these must be mitigated against the pitfalls associated with increased informality.

These insights have a number of implications for theory, method and practice. Theoretically, this article argues that an analysis of informal governance is essential if we are to fully understand how political innovation occurs in practice. Given the in-depth, qualitative and case-specific nature of the study, it is not possible to generalize these findings to other countries, contexts or policy areas. Indeed, most work on informal governance 'takes the form of either abstract theory (N = 0) or inductive case studies (N = 1)' (Helmke and Levitsky 2013, 102). Nonetheless, this case study provides an essential building block for comparison or theory building. This analysis is intended to be a first step in providing an empirical grounding for future analysis on the impact of informal governance on political innovation.

For example, a series of propositions were identified for empirical investigation. Research evidence confirms *Proposition 1: Informal governance creates an 'innovative space' to explore new possibilities and develop trust between critical actors.* Elected politicians had a pivotal role in creating an 'innovative space' for senior administrators to develop new high trust relationships and working practices (Van Tatenhove, Mak, and Liefferink 2006). Back stage, administrators were using informal governance to (re)configure institutional arrangements (Friedman 1995). Evidence also supports *Proposition 2: Informal governance can be used to enhance the autonomy and discretion of administrators, leading to an 'innovative oriented culture'.* This shaped both the intention to be innovative and the creation of a permissive environment for change (Wynen et al. 2014). Informal governance was used by a closely knit group of well-positioned and highly skilled *boundary spanners* (Guarneros-Meza and Martin 2014) who, for the most part, were motivated to use it by cooperative strategies. It was used as a tool to break deadlocks, promote political momentum and complement a weak formal bureaucracy (Lauth 2013). The 'formalization' (Reh 2013) of informal working at critical points was utilized to secure political innovations that had traction.

Finally, research evidence confirms *Proposition 3: Informal governance can lead to more responsive problem solving and a shared commitment to new policy goals.* Central–local relationships were viewed as more collaborative and there was enhanced diversity and creativity in local policy outcomes. However, while informal working was viewed as a route to policy innovation, some respondents acknowledged the negative impacts regards transparency and accountability (Borzel and Panke 2012). Whitehall officials could be accused of using soft power to enforce the 'shadow of hierarchy' in nebulous ways, thus undermining the ability of local actors to secure real influence.

Methodologically, this study confirms that informal governance can be researched at a domestic policy level and that the distinction between formal and informal governance arenas can be identified. Crucially, it also confirms that public managers are willing and able to articulate their views on using informal governance. Indeed, it has been possible to research the 'invisibly' and 'opaque'. Empirically testing a concept like informal governance is challenging and findings are open to interpretation. This is an inevitable feature of in-depth qualitative techniques. While positivist, hypothesis-driven research might be ascribed pre-eminence in some quarters, the findings presented here 'demonstrate once again the valuable insights to be gleaned from qualitative and interpretivist approaches' (Ayres and Marsh 2013, 657). This reinforces the position of world leading governance scholars who have called for greater tolerance in the diversity of theoretical and empirical enquiry and advocate the appropriate use of the full range of available research methods (Rhodes 2013).

Finally, these findings have real value for policymakers and practitioners. Indeed, there was a genuine desire and willingness amongst respondents to articulate, discuss and make sense of the informal world within which they were increasingly operating. At present, there is no policy guidance or research insights to help them take stock, make sense of and then strategically manage informal governance. Indeed, there is much to be gained from pooling shared perceptions, experiences and common behaviours with view to mutual learning, critical reflection and enhancing the capacities of the reflexive practitioner.

Disclosure statement

No potential conflict of interest was reported by the author.

References

Aucoin, P. 2012. "New Political Governance in Westminster Systems: Impartial Public Administration and Management Performance at Risk." *Governance: An International Journal of Policy, Administration and Institutions* 25 (2): 177–199. doi:10.1111/gove.2012.25.issue-2.

Ayres, S., and A. Marsh. 2013. "'Reflections on Contemporary Debates in Policy Studies', Special Issue." *Policy & Politics* 41 (4): 643–663. doi:10.1332/147084413X674001.

Ayres, S., and G. Pearce. 2013. "A Whitehall Perspective on Decentralisation in England's Emerging Territories." *Local Economy* 28 (7–8): 801–816. doi:10.1177/0269094213500631

Borzel, T., and D. Panke. 2012. "'Network Governance: Effective and Legitimate?" In *Theories of Democratic Network Governance*, edited by E. Sørensen and J. Torfing, 153–165. London: Palgrave.

Brie, M., and E. Stolting. 2013. "Formal Institutions and Informal Institutional Arrangements." In *International Handbook on Informal Governance*, edited by T. Christiansen and C. Neuhold, 19–40. Cheltenham: Edward Elgar.

Centre for Public Scrutiny. 2015. *Devo Why? Devo How? Questions (And Some Answers) about Governance under English Devolution*. London: Centre for Public Scrutiny.

Christiansen, T., and C. Neuhold, eds. 2013. *International Handbook on Informal Governance*. Cheltenham: Edward Elgar.

Conservative Party. 2015. *The Conservative Party Manifesto 2015: Strong Leadership, a Clear Economic Plan, a Brighter, More Secure Future*. London: Conservative Party.

Department for Communities and Local Government (DCLG) & the Home Office. 2015. *Cities and Local Government Devolution Bill*. London: The Stationery Office.

Ferreira Da Cruz, N., A. F. Tavares, R. C. Marques, S. Jorge, and L. De Sousa. 2015. "Measuring Local Government Transparency." *Public Management Review*. doi:10.1080/14719037.2015.1051572.

Flinders, M., and M. Wood. 2014. "Depoliticisation, Governance and the State." *Policy & Politics* 42 (2): 135–149. doi:10.1332/030557312X655873.

Friedman, R. 1995. *Front Stage, Backstage: The Dramatic Structure of Labour Negotiations*. Massachusetts: MIT Press.

Fung, A. 2012. "Continuous Institutional Innovation and the Pragmatic Conception of Democracy." *Polity* 44 (4): 609–624. doi:10.1057/pol.2012.17.

Guarneros-Meza, V., and S. Martin (2014) "Boundary Spanning in Local Public Service Partnerships: Coaches, Advocates and Enforcers?" *Public Management Review*, 10.1080/1479037.2014.969761.

Hajer, M. 2003. "Policy without Polity? Policy Analysis and the Institutional Void." *Policy Sciences* 36: 175–195. doi:10.1023/A:1024834510939.

Hambleton, R. 2015. "The Devolution Deception Must Be Exposed." *Local Government Chronicle*. November. http://www.lgcplus.com/politics-and-policy/devolution-and-economic-growth/the-devolution-deception-must-be-exposed/7000578.article

Harsh, M. 2013. "Informal Governance of Emerging Technologies in Africa." In *International Handbook on Informal Governance*, edited by T. Christiansen and C. Neuhold, 481–501. Cheltenham: Edward Elgar.

Hartley, J. 2014. "New Development: Eight and a Half Propositions to Stimulate Frugal Innovation." *Public Money & Management* 34 (3): 227–232. doi:10.1080/09540962.2014.908034.

Hartley, J., E. Sørensen, and J. Torfing. 2013. "Collaborative Innovation: A Viable Alternative to Market Competition and Organizational Entrepreneurship." *Public Administration Review* 73 (6): 821–830. doi:10.1111/puar.2013.73.issue-6.

Helmke, G., and S. Levitsky. 2013. "Informal Institutions and Comparative Politics: A Research Agenda." In *International Handbook on Informal Governance*, edited by T. Christansen and C. Neuhold, 85–117. Cheltenham: Edward Elgar.

Institute for Government. 2014. *Achieving Political Decentralisation: Lessons from 30 Years of Attempting to Devolve Power in the UK*. London: Institute for Government.

Jessop, B. 2016. "Territory, Politics, Governance and Multispatial Metagovernance." *Territory, Politics, Governance* 4 (1): 8–32. doi:10.1080/21622671.2015.1123173.

Jiannan, W., M. Liang, and Y. Yuqian. 2013. "'Innovation in the Chinese Public Sector: Typology and Distribution." *Public Administration* 91 (2): 347–365. doi:10.1111/j.1467-9299.2011.02010.x.

Kickert, W. J. M., E. H. Klijn, and J. F. M. Koppenjan. eds. 1997. *Managing Complex Networks*. London: Sage.

Klijn, E. H. 2014. "Political Leadership in Networks." In *Oxford Handbook of Political Leadership*, edited by R. A. W. Rhodes and P. T Hart, 403–417. Oxford: Oxford University Press.

Klijn, E. H., and J. Koppenjan. 2016. *Governance Networks in the Public Sector*. London: Routledge.

Klijn, E.-H., B. Steijn, and J. Edelenbos. 2010. "The Impact of Network Management Strategies on the Outcomes in Governance Networks." *Public Administration* 88 (4): 1063–1082. doi:10.1111/padm.2010.88.issue-4.

Lane, C., and R. Bachman, eds. 1998. *Trust Within and Between Organisations*. Oxford: Oxford University Press.

Lauth, H. J. 2013. "Informal Governance and Democratic Theory." In *International Handbook on Informal Governance*, edited by T. Christiansen and C. Neuhold, 40–64. Cheltenham: Edward Elgar.

Localis and Grant Thornton. 2015. *Making Devolution Work: A Practical Guide for Local Leaders*. London: Localis and Grant Thornton.

Newman, J. 2012. *Working the Spaces of Power: Activism, Neoliberalism and Gendered Labour*. London: Bloomsbury.

Osborne, S. P., and L. Brown. eds. 2013. *Handbook of Innovations in Public Services*. Cheltenham: Edward Elgar.

Political Studies Association. 2016. *Examining the Role of 'Informal Governance' in Devolution to England's Cities*. London: Political Studies Association.

Polsby, N. 1984. *Political Innovations in America: The Politics of Policy Initiation*. New Haven: Yale University Press.

Reh, C. 2013. "Informal Politics: The Normative Challenge." In *International Handbook on Informal Governance*, edited by T. Christiansen and C. Neuhold, 65–84. Cheltenham: Edward Elgar.

Rhodes, R. A. W. 2013. "Political Anthropology and Civil Service Reform: Prospects and Limits." *Policy & Politics* 41 (4): 481–496. doi:10.1332/030557312X655684.

Rogers, E. 2003. *Diffusion of Innovations*. New York: Free Press.

Sandford, M. 2016. "Devolution to Local Government in England." House of Commons Library Briefing Paper, 07029. April. London: Stationary Office.

Smith, M., and D. Richards. 2015. *Against Ad Hocery: UK Devolution and the Need for Consultation, Consensus and Consideration*. Manchester: University of Manchester.
Sørensen, E. 2016. "Political Innovations: Innovations in political Institutions, Processes and Outputs." *Public Management Review*. doi:10.1080/14719037.2016.1200661.
Torfing, J., B. G. Peters, J. Pierre, and E. Sørensen. 2012. *Interactive Governance: Advancing the Paradigm*. Oxford: Oxford University Press.
van Jitske, P. V., and A. van Buuren. 2015. "Decision Making Patterns in Multilevel Governance: The Contribution of Informal and Procedural Interactions to Significant Multilevel Decisions." *Public Management Review*. doi:10.1080/14719037.2015.1028974.
Van Tatenhove, J., J. Mak, and D. Liefferink. 2006. "The Inter-Play between Formal and Informal Practices." *Perspectives on European Politics and Society* 7 (1): 8–24. doi:10.1080/15705850600839470.
Wynen, J., K. Verhoest, E. Ongaro, and S. Van Thiel. 2014. "Innovation-Oriented Culture in the Public Sector: Do Managerial Autonomy and Result Control Lead to Innovation?" *Public Management Review* 16 (1): 45–66. doi:10.1080/14719037.2013.790273.

Index

Note: **Bold** page numbers refer to tables and *italic* page numbers refer to figures.

advocacy coalition theory 43
aleatoric democracy 21–22; classic idea 22; contribution of 22; research methods 25–26; wicked problems 21
Aleatoric Democracy affects 11
American Tea Party movement 49
Ansell, C. 11
anti-authoritarian revolution 39, 84
anti-authoritarian sentiments 41
Ayres, S. 12

ballot box 13
Bekkers, V. 76
Bischoff, C. S. 11
Borzel, T. 95, 102

cartel party *see* electoral-professional party
Chatham House Rules 97
Christiansen, F. J. 11
climate neutral Utrecht 29
coalition agreement 61
Cohen, M. D. 33
collaborative policy innovation: barriers of 48–50; cases comparison 46, **47**; drivers of 48–50; Gentofte municipality, local task committees 45; New South Wales energy policy 46–48; Venlo regional innovation networks 46
Communities and Local Government (DCLG) 97
community self-organization: research methodology 59–60; theoretical framework 56
councillors roles: federation and local government 63–65; governance experiment 60–61, 63; joint vision development 65; political pressures 65–66; public–private–society partnership 66–67
creative destruction 5

Danish Parliament 11, 40
Danish People's Party 80
Danish political system 85
DCLG *see* Department for Communities and Local Government (DCLG)
democracy models: framework-setting role 58; participatory view of 56–57; politicians roles 57–59, **59**; representative form of 56; self-organizing view of 57
democratic arrangement 36
democratic systems: citizens representative group 22; elements of 22; mini-publics 21, 22; political innovations 20, 23, 33
Department for Communities and Local Government (DCLG) 98, 100
De Vries, H. 76
de Vries, J. P. 11
Dryzek, J. S. 22

Edelenbos, J. 11
educational revolution 39
elected politicians: anti-authoritarian sentiments 41; enabled informatization 40; ongoing mediatization 40; real-life policy problems 41
Election Day 75, 78
electoral cycles 8, 12, 69, 70
electoral-professional party 78
Energy Plan 2016–2030 26
EUROCITIES Award 25
European party systems 84

Faber, A. 11
Friedman, R. 93, 94

G1000, aleatoric democracy 28
Goodin, R. E. 22

INDEX

Hajer, M. 91, 97
Hall, P. A. 42
hamper political systems 4
hard power 41
Harmel, R. 78
Helms, L. 51, 75, 79
Hupe, P. 3

informal governance: advantages 97; the arenas **96**, 96–97; definition 95; devolution debate 91; disadvantages 97; hypothesis-driven research 104; impact of 99, **99**; institutional void 99; literature review 93–97; the motives 96, **96**; operationalizing 95–97; policy background 92–93; research methods 97; solve policy problems 91; wicked problems 91
innovation theory 3, 34
inspire innovations 5
interactions 81–83

Janda, C. 78
Jenkins-Smith, H. C. 44
Jessop, B. 7, 12
Jochim, A. E. 40
Jones, B. D. 40

Kingdon, J. W. 42, 43
Kingdon, R. 3
Koppenjan, J. 11
Krouwel, A. 79

Laclau, E. 6
Liberal–Democrats 26, 27, 29, 32
Liefferink, D. 95, 96
Lijphart, A. 83
linkage 78–80
Lipset, M. 84
Locke, John 23

Machiavelli, Niccolò 21
Mair, P. 82
Mak, J. 95, 96
March, J. G. 33
Meier, K. J. 40
Meijer, A. J. 11
Mill, John Stuart 21
mini-publics 21, 22
modern Western societies 7
Montesquieu 21, 23
multi-level political system 10
multiparty systems 82
multi-polity policymaking 7

neoliberal economic policies 40
new public management reforms 3

Olsen, J. P. 33

PAC *see* Public Accounts Committee (PAC)
Panke, D. 95, 102
Pierson, P. 12
Pitkin, H. 77
policy 84–85
policy innovations 9–10; crucial role 43; data analysis 101–103; data findings 101–103; limited role in 50; literature review 94–95; multi-actor collaboration 44; new political agendas 42; studies of 41–44; vehicles of 43
political contestation and majoritarian system 8
political debate 22, 40, 71
Political Innovation in America 42
political innovation process: barriers 67–70; citizen initiative Broekpolder 60, *62*; contemporary representative democracies 6; creative destruction 5; drivers 67–70; existing policies 4; implementation of 24; institutional context 25; interrelatedness between 10–12; literature review 93–97; multi-level political system 8; negative outcomes 5; in policy 9–10; politicians roles 67, **68**; in politics 8–9; prominent issue 8; promoting public innovation 12–13; proposed governance model 60, *61*; public innovation research programme 4; selection 24; stepby-step innovations 5; theoretical framework 56; three forms 6
political leadership: anti-authoritarian revolution 39; anti-authoritarian sentiments 41; educational revolution 39; enabled informatization 40; frequent and systematic engagement of 38; hard power 41; innovative policy solutions 38; mediatization of 40; out-of-the-box solutions 37; soft power 41; studies of 41–44; three crucial functions 41–42; Western societies 39–41
political parties structure: economic and social problems 82; public demands 75; theoretical typology 75; 'wicked' problems 79
political parties typology: individual and collective roles 76; interactions 81–83; linkage 78–80; party systems 76; policy 84–85; policy-making process 77;

programme 80–81; representation concepts 76–77
political system: Danish political system 93; innovation capacity of 6; issue machine 65; new ideas 22–24; policy innovation capacity 12; policy-making capacity of 78; public innovation agenda 12; strategic component 22–24; of United States 85; votes and power play 71
politics innovations 7–8, 8–9; data analysis 99–101; data findings 99–101; literature review 94
polity innovations: data analysis 97–99; data findings 97–99; literature review 93–94
Pollitt, C. 3
post-industrial society 78
presidentialization 79
programme 80–81
protective democracy model 57
Public Accounts Committee (PAC) 46
public innovation research programme 4
public sector innovations: innovations types 4, 5; open-ended studies 4; problem-solving capacity 3; service-oriented approach 4

radical innovations 5
Richards, D. 101
Rogers, E. M. 76
Rokkan, S. 84
Rousseau, Jean-Jacques 21, 23

Sabatier, P. A. 44
Sartori, G. 81

Schumpeter, J. 5
Smith, M. 101
soft power 41, 94
Sørensen, E. 33, 58, 74, 75, 76, 90, 91

Torfing, J. 11, 58, 76
Torfing, J. B. G. 93
trigger innovations 5, 20
Tucker, R. C. 41
Tummers, L. 76

US Congress 42, 83
Utrecht's plan: coalition plans 32; deliberative method 29; Energy Plan 2016–2030 26; institutional context 31–32; political innovation implementation 29–30; political innovation selection 28–29; silent majority 28; wind power development plans 27

van der Veer, R, 11
van Meerkerk, I. 11
van Reybrouck, D. 28
Van Tatenhove, J. 95, 96
Venlo Greenport Project 46
veto-player theory 83
Von Clausewitz, Carl 21

western democratic models 20
Western European party systems 84
Whitehall's Cabinet Committee 98
wicked problems 21, 29, 41, 87, 99
Workman, S. 40